The Vocabulary Project

All the Words You Should Have Looked Up in College...and Beyond

Kentworth Edel

IronwoodHill Press, Riverside, NJ

Copyright 2004, Kentworth M. Edel
All rights reserved.

ISBN-10: 061535465-3
ISBN-13: 978-0-615-35465-1

All examples of usage herein are by the author, unless otherwise attributed.

Inquiries and comments may be directed to: editor@ironwoodhillpress.com.

For Megeen

Contents

Preface — 1

Introduction — 3

Using This Book — 13

The Vocabulary — 19

Index — 227

Preface

This is a vocabulary book, but a special one. It answers the question, "what words could I, a reasonably intelligent and literate person, have added to my vocabulary over the years if I had paid better attention?" Contained here are all of the words that I (another reasonably intelligent and literate person) stumbled upon while in college, and in thirty-some years beyond college, whose meaning I either did not know or was unsure of. My study of the earliest of these words led directly to my scoring 100% on the vocabulary sections of both the MCAT and the GRE tests.

I present the nearly 1300 words here largely in the order in which I encountered them, and so they naturally become more obscure as one treads farther into the book. As tedious as the prospect of studying them might appear, the payoff for the reader is that the more common words, and thereby the more useful, are toward the front: if you abandon the effort early, you still get a lot of bang for your efforts.

Introduction

A few months into my freshman year of college, I became suddenly and urgently inspired to act on some advice that surely all of us received early and often from our grade-school teachers: if you don't know what a word means, look it up! Certainly I was no more energetic than the average freshman, but a motivating notion had struck me that perhaps had missed some of the other kids who were in the same quandary that I was in. This motivating notion was my sudden perception—wrong though it turned out to be—that if I did not get into medical school three years hence, my life would be over. And the quandary was this: in two short years my fellow wanna-be medical students and I would have to take the dreaded MCAT: the Medical College Admission Test.

In one intense session, this little five-hour inquisition would be testing our achievement levels in math, general knowledge, science, and English vocabulary. Recognizing that my admission to medical schools would be impossible if I flubbed this test, I put some hard thought into how I might get an edge on the competition—for a competition it unquestionably was. I rapidly concluded that there was little extra activity I could undertake in order to strengthen my general knowledge, my math ability, and my science knowledge. Surely my youthful lifetime of regular reading, as aimless as it was, had already given me most of the general knowledge I would possess by the time of the test. (And was it even feasible at this point to study "general knowledge"? What a broad subject!) Moreover, in the next two years of classes it was certain that I would learn or re-learn most of the required science and math. So that left just one area in which I could improve my MCAT score through some organized course of study that wouldn't consume all of my free time: vocabulary.

Lit up now by this notion that my ticket into medical school was a bigger vocabulary, I became obsessed with acquiring one, and this is what I devised as a plan: every time I came across a word I didn't know, I would write it down and then look it up—following the advice, years late, of those wise teachers. In practice, though, my new compulsion grew to be a little more methodical. Realizing that I could not tote my heavy dictionary around with me, and only too aware of the tedium associated with looking up a word, in those pre-personal-computer days, I settled upon a workable routine. Each time I came across a new word I would write it down on a little piece of paper, actually tearing a piece out of whatever notebook I had with me or using a corner from a newspaper page. I hit upon this idea of using paper scraps (this was before the advent of Post-It Notes) because early on I found myself forgetting where I had written down words. I figured that if they were written on little pieces of paper, then I could simply look for them in my pockets. So at the end of a typical day I would arrive back at my dorm room with several of these paper scraps, and I would toss them into a bowl on my desk. Then on Friday evenings—pathetically, one might say—I would record them in a notebook, look them up, and write down their definitions. I resolved to keep this up relentlessly until I took the MCAT in the spring of my junior year.

Not surprisingly, after a couple months of this routine I started to notice some trends. First, I was encountering a lot of words that actually were familiar to me, but I had to admit that I did not know what they meant. This implied that in the course of my normal reading I had been glossing over these words uncomprehendingly. Context be damned—I didn't have a clue about their meaning. Second, where at the beginning I was writing down at least five words a day, within a month or so I was down to maybe two: simply in the course of defining the words—not consciously trying to memorize them—I was internalizing them enough so that when I came across them again, I knew they were already in my notebook. Finally, once I had written down a word I suddenly saw it everywhere. This last observation in particular got me wondering just what I had been missing in the course of my reading. This emerging notion—that ultimately I was acting to enrich my reading experience—was an unforeseen dividend of my study, whose motivation up till now I will admit had been somewhat crass.

Two years later, in the middle of my junior year, paranoia crept in. Although I was at a point where I was gathering just two or three words a week, I was nevertheless tormented by the nagging thought that there was another large set of vocabulary out there that I had somehow missed. As much as I feared confronting this hobgoblin, I recognized that I nevertheless must do so in order to walk into the MCAT testing room with confidence. So one day I found myself in my college bookstore with the daunting and half-imagined plan of reading through every vocabulary book on the rack. I will admit to some trepidation here, since this exercise could very well have shown me that all my diligent efforts had been grossly insufficient. The upshot, however, was that after an hour spent perusing several books, I had run across only one new word—which I promptly wrote down on a little scrap of paper. Then, with just a few dollars to my name and desperately needing to buy a pack of smokes (this was 1975, when they cost forty cents in the machine), I swallowed hard and burned a couple of bucks on a shrink-wrapped pack of vocabulary flash cards. Minutes later, standing outside the bookstore and acting very much like some other breed of addict, I ripped open the pack and warily flipped through the cards. I knew every word.

A few weeks later I took the MCAT. I got bruised a bit in the science, general knowledge, and math portions, for although I was no slouch, I was competing against a selective crowd. But in the vocabulary section I did not encounter a single word that was unknown to me. I scored in the 99th percentile in the vocabulary section—the highest that one can score—and this fact pulled up my rank for the overall test to the 96th percentile.

As it turned out, my future did not lie in medicine, but this change had nothing to do with my MCAT score—for after all I performed better than 96 percent of the other applicants. And—surprising to me—instead of abandoning my word quest after taking the MCAT as I had always planned, I continued this practice of writing down unknown words (in that same notebook) and defining them. As a testament to the early part of that continuing effort: by the time I took the Graduate Record Examination (GRE) a year after I graduated and two years after the MCAT, I had picked up a couple of hundred more words. On the GRE's verbal portion, which in those days was largely a vocabulary test, I scored 830 out of 800—breaking the test, as far as I can tell—and again, as in the MCAT, none of the words was unknown to me.

What I Had Been Reading

It might be surprising that in the few years leading up to these tests I was not reading anything unusual. Like most college students, I would read my college's newspaper every weekday. As a diversion from studying, I would spend part of an odd afternoon now and then reading the glossy magazines in my dorm's cool, quiet, and lonely little library: *The New Yorker, Harper's, Atlantic Monthly, National Review, Saturday Review* (back when it was a literary magazine...), *Commentary, American Spectator, The Nation, Mother Jones, National Lampoon*—but reading only the articles that were interesting to me. And mindful of my obligation to read as much of the English Lit. canon as I could during these college years, I was usually reading a novel as well. It is instructive to note that these words I was writing down in my college years were not particularly obscure words, since they were obviously in use by writers who were reaching contemporary and broad audiences.

Thirty-some years older now and still on the lookout for unacquired words, I find that I no longer encounter them in the course of popular reading—newspapers, light fiction, and newsmagazines. The new words tend rather to be in places where the writer is counting on the high expectations of his audience that words will be chosen for their ability to precisely convey the thought. Christopher Hitchens, Camille Paglia, the late William F. Buckley, and Cormac McCarthy come to mind here, as they are writers whose audiences come to them fully expecting to be dazzled by an unusually rich—and well-employed—diction.

Why Acquire a Larger Vocabulary

What is a big word? For certain, it is usually not big: most of the more obscure words in this book—say, the ones in the last fourth—are actually short. So when we commonly say "big words," we really are talking about those words that simply are not known to most people. With some justified uncertainty it is natural to ask whether there is any real benefit to knowing these words. Baldly exploiting this uncertainty are advertisements that we often see, pestering us to buy vocabulary-building products that aim—or claim—to speed our rise up the corporate ladder or make us seem brighter. But my own hard experience in big corporations and among social groups tells me that if you use a word that is uncommon, even if it is known to your audience, it can mark you as a pretender and a show-off. Or—worst of all—it marks you as somebody who is so out of touch that he thinks everybody else understands what "decretal" means. I recall with some lingering embarrassment that in my late twenties I used the word "ineluctable" in a business memo, and I am still grateful to a blunt, well-meaning, and wise older manager whom I had copied on the memo: he took me aside and advised me never to do that again.

A common saying is that you should never use a dollar word when a nickel word will do, and I cannot argue with that. The essence of glibness is to be able to express your thoughts without struggling—that is, without having to stop in mid-sentence to search for some word that you rarely use. When instead you habitually use a fundamental and common vocabulary, the words are right there in your head when you look for them. But there is nevertheless a singular and continuing benefit from having a larger vocabulary: it allows us to more richly enjoy what we read and hear, period. (Buckley once compared it to the way a learned musician might get more enjoyment from a jazz or symphonic piece than a dilettante would.) Maybe from time to time, when we face a certain audience, we can be justified in using that big word that more nearly expresses our thoughts in the most efficient way. And when we have that perfect audience—a group of university professors or magazine editors are ones that come to mind, and I honestly cannot think of many others—then we can joyfully uncloak our full vocabulary and let them have it.

What is Unique about this Vocabulary Book

All vocabulary books seem to put their words in some sort of methodical order. This one is arranged methodically, too: as I mentioned in my preface, the fourteen hundred words here generally appear in the order in which I encountered them. As a result, the earlier words are more common, and the later ones are more obscure. In this way, perhaps the reader who bails out after one third of the book will have gotten two thirds of the benefit, if his goal is to internalize a reading vocabulary that gets him through popular literature without missing much.

Commonly, the contents of vocabulary books tend to be organized by categories: for example, by broad groups of meaning (rather like a Thesaurus) or by groups of words derived from one ancient language or another, or by groups of words that might be encountered in particular contexts. Some of these books might seem a little dumbed-down in that they present words that most literate folks would already know, or they might mix it up by grouping these more common words with ones that you probably would never use. But you would have to read each of these books in their entirety in order to acquire even the more common of any unknown words—and indeed you might have trouble memorizing the distinctions among words when they are presented to you in groupings. This book, uniquely I think, is arranged to provide you the biggest payoff for your time spent, regardless of how far into it you actually read.

Which Words Are Included Here, and Why

My aim is to show two (necessarily) overlapping sets of words that form a continuum from most common to most obscure:

> 1. **Words that are in the "college vocabulary,"** i.e. those that a college student might encounter anew during those four years; these words compose roughly the first two thirds of the book.

2. **Words that I consider to be in the "post-graduate vocabulary,"** i.e. the more obscure words that one might not have encountered in normal college reading. (Lest one question whether the order of these words might really be significant, consider this fact: it took four years for me to find the first 650 words, and thirty years to find the next 650.)

In places, I have massaged the order of these words just a bit from the order in which I first acquired them, for several reasons: by chance there were words 1 encountered early in my study that actually were fairly obscure, according to my later judgment, and these I have pushed toward the rear. It also occurred to me that every college freshman—even one with a sub-normal vocabulary—arrives at school possessing a small "extra-normal" set of words, peculiar to him for one reason or another, that might be beyond the normal high-school vocabulary of other freshmen. For just this reason, the words in my own peculiar extra-normal set never made it into my notebook, as I had never had to write them down. So over the last few years while preparing this book, I have been on the alert for these words and have inserted them into the book where I think they belong. [As one example: when I was seven or eight, my mother was teaching a junior-college course in business English; I distinctly remember opening her textbook one day and reading the word "abeyance" there, along with its definition—which for some reason I memorized. So that obscure word inhabited my vocabulary when I was a college freshman, although it had no business being there—nor in a business-English class, for that matter! I have placed it in the last third of this book.]

Further, I have intentionally left out words that I personally deem to be part of the normal college-bound high-school graduate's vocabulary: for example, "admonish, "contrive," "requisite," "heretofore," "ubiquitous," "obliterate," "serendipity," "condescend." These might not be in a college-bound high-school student's active *speaking* vocabulary, but I think he would know these words when he reads them. This is a matter of personal, not academic, opinion, and I can go by no other measure than to assume that my own vocabulary at 18 was no better or worse than the average college-bound high-school graduate's.

Over the thirty-five-year course of my project I recorded perhaps twenty words that have no definition that I can find, and I have tossed these. Some of them appear to have been misspellings: "peragic," for example, gleaned from a cheap paperback edition of *Moby Dick*. I have not been able to uncover its definition, and I suspect that the word was a typesetter's misreading of "pelagic" (itself an obscure word meaning "of or relating to the open sea"). I have reasoned that if I these words are not to be found in mid-sized Webster's or American Heritage dictionaries, then they are not in common usage and do not belong here (nor for that matter on a vocabulary test!).

I have excluded also technical terms and words peculiar to certain areas of hobby, expertise, or industry—for example, "anthracite," "kluge," "bodkin," "quark," and "catharpins." Also, with just a few exceptions I have left out foreign words, i.e. ones that you still see italicized when they are encountered (and which might have been intended as a pedantic in-joke by their authors). I made these exceptions because—as exemplified by the German *"schadenfreude"*—they say in one word what is impossible to say in English without using an entire phrase; I am sure that there are many English words which do the same for other languages. Lastly: in places I have moved one word next to another to suit the purposes of comparison or completeness.

Using This Book

This is not a dictionary—it is a vocabulary book. You would use a dictionary to find the meaning of a particular word, and so topic words appear there in alphabetical order. You use this book, rather, to acquire new vocabulary: you would not routinely consult it in order to look up any particular word that you have in mind, for its topic words are not in alphabetical order, nor does it discuss etymology and provide extensive definitions. I have included an index so that one can check to see if any particular word appears here, although I can imagine someone's doing so only for academic reasons: if you do have a particular word in mind, you already know of its existence and do not need to hunt here merely for its definition!

    A vocabulary book needs to do two things: first, it has to ease the drudgery of looking up the new words that it lists, so it has to have the defining done for you already. And second, it has to present you with the right words (note that I have explained in the Introduction how the words here were chosen). The problem with using a dictionary as a vocabulary book is that it presents us with lots of words that we already know, in addition to showing us far, far more words that most of us will never need to know (for example, the names of all the parts of a crossbow).

    I have heard that there is a time in a toddler's life when he learns hundreds of words each day. This does not mean that he newly encounters hundreds of words each day—for that would be contrary to experience. What is happening, rather, is that the toddler has reached a point where words he has heard a thousand times before somehow gel suddenly into permanent meaning somewhere in his brain, and apparently at some point it happens with hundreds of words at a time. I don't think we ever lose this ability: I recall a graduate student I knew in college who took a summer crash course in Chinese vocabulary in which he had to learn 50 words a day for three weeks. These were mostly common words that he had come across already in his prior studies of Chinese language but hadn't really internalized—and he did learn them. Similarly, people in immersion-language courses commonly report that one day they find they possess a speaking vocabulary that they didn't have the day before. The common thread here is that there are lots of words you are already familiar with but do not know—and it is possible to add a large body of words to your vocabulary in a short period of time.

So—if you want to learn a lot of words quickly, I don't believe you can do it in the old "word a day" manner: that requires too much discipline and long-term commitment for most of us, and you accumulate words so slowly that you don't get the full benefit until you have aged a few years. In my own case, it turned out that in the two years leading up to the MCAT, I did not mount any attempt at all to study my list of words until a few weeks before the test; for all my discipline in having energetically defined the words every week, I was nevertheless too lazy to study them afterwards. I recall having studied them only once, on a holiday in which I read the list through several times. I never studied it again before the test—but I will admit that I had the advantage of once having had to grind through the looking up of every word, so no doubt my subconscious had already picked them up to some extent.

I cannot presume to tell anybody how best to memorize a large set of vocabulary. But I think my own example is illustrative: one good way to use this book is simply to read through it. You might find it interesting to see how many of these words are actually familiar—and to see how their definitions might be different from what you suspected they were (as was often the case when I sat down to define them). And as you near the end of the book, you might find it almost laughable, as I did, that some contemporary writers apparently are deeming the use of such obscure words justifiable. But then you are gratified, when you read a particular example of usage, that the author was well justified in choosing precisely that word after all.

Format of the Articles

I have tried to keep each definition short, where possible, so that you can read just the first line in each article to get it. Each article is arranged in the following format:

> **word** (or **alternate spelling**)
> definition; second definition: synonym maybe. (Commentary on usage. Perhaps a note on other inflections of the word, if warranted.) "Example sentence in which the word is used." [Attribution, unless I wrote the example sentence.]

Not all of these elements are necessarily used in each article. Here is one example:

> **bemused**
> bewildered, dazed, or lost in thought, as if affected by one's muse: thoughtful. (This is not a synonym for "amused," although newspaper

writers and TV reporters seem to use it that way nowadays with disturbing frequency. Best used when you know it will not be misinterpreted — let context guide its impact.) "Her lover had departed without his usual blown kiss, and she gazed, bemused, at the wilted bouquet she had forgotten to put into water the night before."

Resources

In defining these words I chiefly have consulted the following-listed three dictionary sources and amended their definitions as I have seen fit, based on my view of common context. As a rule I have consulted the *Oxford English Dictionary* in cases where the first two sources have clashed a bit, or when a word is not to be found in them.

Webster's Seventh New Collegiate Dictionary. G. & C. Merriam, 1970.

American Heritage Dictionary of the English Language, Third Edition. Houghton-Mifflin, 1992.

The Oxford English Dictionary, 2nd Edition. Clarendon Press, Oxford, 1989.

The Vocabulary

parlous
hazardous, perilous. "Sen. Barack Obama...addressed one of the key issues, the parlous state of the government-sponsored buyer of mortgages." [Bob Davis and T.W. Farnam, "Shaky Economy Challenges Ambitious Obama Agenda," *Wall Street Journal*.]

splenetic
tending toward melancholy or ill humor. (See also *crotchety* . Splenetic people need—figuratively—to vent their spleen.)

pusillanimous
lacking courage, tentative: cowardly. "In 1931, British Prime Minister Stanley Baldwin, known for his vehement pusillanimity...explained why he was certain that complete disarmament was the only solution." [Algis Valiunas, "Fire from the Sky," *Commentary*.]

poltroon
a base and contemptible coward. " I'm talking about the timid, walking-on-eggshells, pusillanimous poltroons that dominate modern politics." [Arianna Huffington, "Al Gore Overcomes the Fear Factor, Hillary Suc-

cumbs," *The Huffington Post*. (Note: Ms. Huffington is by no means the first writer to use the phrase, "pusillanimous poltroon.")]

allusion

an indirect reference, in speech or writing, to an external event or thing. "His little aside on the sanctity of marriage was obviously a snide allusion to my several divorces."

benignant

gentle and beneficial; kind and gracious. (This is generally the opposite of "malignant.") "It always surprised me that the bear in that TV series, *Gentle Ben*—being so often scolded and admonished by that pudgy little actor—was always more benignant than he was bent on satisfying his hunger for fresh meat."

malign

(as an adjective) evil, intending to do harm, malevolent. "They are joined, in a sinister perversion of Burke, by 'realists' who argue that traditional culture is so powerful and so malign that the region must be left to stew in its juices." [Richard Brookhiser, "Tories and Radicals," *New York Times Sunday Book Review*.]

placate

to make another person calm or less angry or placid, especially by offerings; to pacify. "...an offering to placate the gods."

enigmatic

obscure, inexplicable, and sort of mysterious. [There are lots of words like this—all included in this book—that describe something not often seen or not easily seen, and they all have different flavors of the concept: see also *esoteric* (understood by a few), *cabalistic* (peculiar to a group of plotters), *arcane* (understood by the few who are in certain professions or pursuits), *inscrutable* (nearly impossible to figure out, due to its lack of obvious features), *inchoate* (just formed, barely expressed), *abstruse* (poorly expressed), *recondite* (cloaked; not clearly expressed but not meant to be either), *opaque* (unintelligible ("not passing light")), *impalpable* (not touchable), *noumenal* (not of the physical world), *cryptic* (in need of deciphering); *turbid* (unintelligible(cloudy)).]

pellucid

clear, especially in meaning; readily understandable; passing light. (A close relative of *perspicuous* (not *perspicacious*!).) "It's a pellucid, well-reasoned argument...but I don't agree with it.]

diffident

appearing reserved and shy; cautiously timid. "The passengers are a diffident lot; they cage their eyes and no man asks another what it is that brings him here." [Cormac McCarthy, *Blood Meridian*.]

ineluctable

not to be changed, avoided, escaped, or resisted. (This is not really a synonym for *inevitable*. Income taxes are ineluctable, whereas the frustration that comes from dealing with the tax is inevitable. The first we must accept, but the second we can perhaps fight.) "On the other hand, the strength of support among Hong Kong's younger citizens...shows that time is not ineluctably on Beijing's side." [John Bolton, "What the President Can Learn from Google," *The Wall Street Journal*.]

cryptic
> seemingly in code; hard to decipher; mystifying. "Early researchers had concentrated on interpreting Kahn's work either in terms of his own cryptic theoretical pronouncements or else in terms of its relationship to the broad professional and cultural currents of the day." [Michael J. Lewis, "The Gregarious Loner," *Commentary*.]

esurient
> greedy, hungry. (Accent on the second syllable.)

esoteric
> designed for or understood only by people who share the same technology, interest, birthright, profession, etc. "And it's true that there is something insufferably esoteric about the whole notion of *Grindhouse*... but is it all, perhaps, one big elaborate in-joke too many?" [Kevin Maher, "Has Tarantino Been Flushed Away?" *TimesOnline*.]

loath (or **loth**)
> not inclined; reluctant. (Not to be confused with *loathe*.) "For Edward, much time is lost in bitterly recalling the frozen attitude of the loth maiden and replaying the moment of desolate frustration." [Christopher Hitchens, "Think of England," *The Atlantic*.]

loathe
> to despise, to strongly dislike and reject; abhor. "Funny thing–I loathe sushi, but I love it once it's cooked."

calumnious
> slanderous. (Noun form is *calumny*.)

querulous
    habitually complaining or finding fault: peevish. "As my aging mother lost control of her finances and her day-to-day decisions, she became reluctantly dependent on me and understandably querulous."

ebullient
    lively, enthusiastic, full of the moment, zesty.

sanative
    having a healing effect. "The best thing about having a cold is that one is totally justified in crawling into bed with a sanative glass of neat scotch."

capricious
    apt to change unpredictably; subject to whim. Noun is *caprice*.

vapid
    lacking content, liveliness, tang, force, vigor, zest: dull. "He would despise the title Citizen of the World for its vapidity." [Paul Greenberg, "Naipaul's Nobel: The Eye of Exile," *Jewish World Review*.] "...a vapid, dreary man whose interests ranged from afternoon TV to the next meal."

peculator
    one who embezzles.

canaille
    (as a noun) riffraff, unclean or shabby people, the lower class; (as an adjective) pertaining to the lower class.

indolent

disinclined to exert oneself; lazy and lethargic; causing such. Noun is *indolence*. "He fell silent again, riding beside me, easy and indolent in the saddle." [Owen Wister, *The Virginian*.]

vivacious

lively, spirited, full of life. "...being the vivacious sort, she tended to be in the center of the room wherever she stood."

denouement

the final outcome; the resolution of a story or plot. Often italicized as a French word and pronounced so.

paragon

a model of excellence, or the most nearly perfect state of a kind of thing. A hackneyed usage is "a paragon of virtue." This is not to be confused with *paradigm*.

paradigm

a pattern of outlook or of world-view; a modus operandi; something that serves as a model. "Paradigm shift" is a hackneyed usage, although useful.

voluble

speaking with a ready ease. Not to be confused with *verbose*.

verbose

tending to use more words than necessary to express a thought: wordy.

tenuous

uncertain, flimsy. "...even a minor disruption or dislocation of one of the existing key Iranian sites could have the effect of retarding the whole tenuous program for quite a while." [Christopher Hitchens, "Why Wait to Disarm Iran?," *Slate.com*.]

academe

the academic community as a whole, academic environment. "Halls of academe" is a hackneyed usage.

cabalistic

relating to a traditional secret, usually of a group of people or a sect. "Cabalistic rituals" is a hackneyed use. See below—its noun (*cabal*) is a little different.

cabal

a group of plotters or conspirators.

travesty

a grotesque or especially unfaithful translation or interpretation. A trite phrase is "travesty of justice." This is often used ignorantly as a synonym for *tragedy*; that usage would itself be a travesty.

prurient

of or appealing to an uncalled-for or inordinate interest in sex. "Prurient interests" is a hackneyed usage. "The supposedly "broad-minded" culture turns out to be as prurient and salacious as the elders in *The Scarlet Letter*." [Christopher Hitchens, "Siege of Paris," *Slate.com*.]

The Vocabulary 25

acrimonious

caustic, biting, or bitter in manner, tone, and/or feeling. A common phrase is "acrimonious debate," but perhaps the word is better applied to the participants.

proclivity

an inherent inclination, usually toward a vice or something objectionable. See *propensity*. Not to be confused with *declivity* (a downward slope...).

miscegenate

to intermarry, to mix races. *Miscegenation* is the noun.

ascetic

as an adjective: austere in habit, practicing strict self-denial; having renounced pleasurable things. Not to be confused with "acidic," which it sounds like if not carefully pronounced! As a noun: one who has renounced pleasures, as in "religious ascetic," i.e. one whose practice of religion is ascetic.

fecund

fertile, having or capable of having a lot of offspring. *Fecundity* is the noun. Pronounced "feecund."

salacious

arousing sexual desire or thoughts, or appealing to same: *lascivious*. See *concupiscent* for a word that describes one in whose brain these thoughts are aroused.

puffery
> excessive praise. "Much press coverage of the President's Middle East campaign trip was Soviet-style puffery of the first order."

beleaguer
> to beset or harrass; to surround (as in battle). "She looked...into the eyes in the glass as if it were some sister there who weathered stoically this beleaguerment of her hopes. [Cormac McCarthy, *Cities of the Plain*.]

onerous
> imposing or constituting a burden; oppressive. An *onus* is a burden or obligation.

efface
> to wipe out, obliterate, erase. "Self-effacing" is a hackneyed usage, i.e. a self-effacing person minimizes or denies his successes and achievements.

sordid
> morally debased; base and vulgar; characterized by an attachment or interest in baser elements. "There is of course the powerful institutional interest that the U.S. State Department has in concealing some of his more sordid actions." [Sukumar Muralidharan, "A Bill of Indictment," *The Hindu*.]

accoutrements (or **accouterments**)
> extra items of clothing or accessories necessary to a function or task; trappings; outward signs that allow one to recognize something. Nearly always encountered in the plural. "When I saw her driving the Jag, I rec-

ognized that she finally had all the proper accoutrements of a kept woman."

abnegate

to surrender or relinquish (something intangible); to deny, renounce. "When she joined the Moonies, she at once abnegated both the world she saw as unjust, and the company of people whose only sin was to love her unselfishly."

contumacy

rebellion, obstinate insubordination, contemptuous opposition to authority. Accent on the first syllable.

exacerbate

to make more severe, bitter, unpleasant, violent, or undesirable: to aggravate or worsen. "Many parents are afraid that the enforcing of rules will only exacerbate their children's unruliness."

promulgate

to make known, or to put into effect, especially by public pronouncement. A plan is promulgated, as is an agenda. Accent on "prom."

perspicacious

having unusually keen or penetrating powers of mental perception; not to be confused with *perspicuous*.

perspicuous

easily or readily understandable. Not to be confused with *perspicacious*. See *pellucid, percipient*.

angst

anxiety or despair, accompanied perhaps by depression or gloom. This is a popular affliction among the protagonists of twentieth-century existential novelists, as in *existential angst;* brought about, one supposes, by the hero's perceiving too finely that he is the only one, among all his acquaintances, who really understands that life is merely a futile quest for immortality.

putative

thought to be; supposed. A criminal who is thought by reporters to head up a larger criminal organization than those run by the crooks they routinely come into contact with is commonly referred to as a "putative crime boss."

temerity

impudence, cheekiness; foolish disregard for danger. Often used facetiously, where the act described is really one of forthrightness but is viewed by one's opponent as cheek. "The final straw was her temerity to make her primary race about her opponent's Washington earmarking record." [Kimberley A. Strassel, "GOP Reformers Face a Tough Fight," *Wall Street Journal.*]

facetious

intended to be serious or valid only on the surface, as in certain comments. (Example: "Wow, nice dog," said when one is being barked at.) "Facetiousness is the little brother of sarcasm, which is facetiousness intended to cut."

The Vocabulary 29

panache

verve, flair, dash; exhibiting a high and exuberant style. "In some professions—advertising or architecture, for example—wearing the skinny end of your tie in front would mean you had a lot of panache; in most others however it would be a travesty of decorum."

pertinacious

obstinate, exasperatingly persistent in holding onto a belief or course of action.

termagant

agitatedly boisterous and/or scolding. As a noun, it refers to a woman who is quarrelsome and looking for a brawl. Accent on the first syllable.

eclectic

selected from, or selecting from, the best from among a wide variety of tastes or sources. This is over-used nowadays by fashion writers and interior designers: they always say you're eclectic if they can't honestly say anything good about your wretched taste. "Michael Jackson's evolving facial features reflected the eclectic nature of his insecurities."

epiphany

a sudden understanding of some profound or essential truth. "It's a high moment for the Wodehouse style; an epiphany, if you must, to be compared with King Lear's reflections on his own considerable reverses of fortune." [Alexander Cockburn in an introduction to P.G. Wodehouse's *The Code of the Woosters*.]

iconoclastic
   attacking or looking to overthrow accepted norms, institutions, or standards: icon-busting. Noun is *iconoclast*. "Suggesting a workable, plausible, and viable alternative is a burden that most iconoclasts are too cool to shoulder."

unctuous (also **unctious**)
   being too suave or having the pretense of righteousness, having an exaggerated interest or earnestness; oiliness. "Perhaps global-scale problems and mass-society populism somehow necessitate this unctuous appeal to the utter specialness of the supposed individual." [Christopher Hitchens, "The You Decade," *Slate.com*.]

demur
   to voice an objection or opposing view. (Not to be confused with *demure*.). "At that point in the discussion we thought we were uanimous, but then Charlie demurred."

demure
   shy, modestly reserved.

codocil
   something added to a document, as a further provision or an appendix. Wills usually have codocils attached, as do lending agreements.

moribund
   near death, or dying. Used more often to describe many inanimate things also, like political systems, philosophies, etc. "...Ferdinand de Saussure, the granddaddy of now mercifully moribund post-structuralism, which

destroyed American humanities departments in the 1980s." [Camille Paglia, "Pelosi's Victory for Women," *Salon.com*.]

bemused

bewildered, dazed, or lost in thought, as if affected by one's muse: thoughtful. (This is not a synonym for "amused," although newspaper writers and TV reporters use it that way with disturbing frequency. Best used when you know it will not be misinterpreted — let context guide its impact.) "Her lover had departed without his usual blown kiss, and she gazed, bemused, at the wilted bouquet she had forgotten to put in water the night before."

sybaritic

reflecting a love of luxury, especially to the point of dissipation. "Even if we do not consider a fountain in one's living room to be a luxury (for it might well be a pain in the butt!), it still reflects the sybaritic propensities of its owner."

austere

severe, harsh, stern; extremely plain and bare. "The problem with former presidents is that knowing them keeps you from being awed by the presidency. When you haven't met them, you have a more austere and august sense of who they are, and what a president is." [Peggy Noonan, "The Incredible Shrinking Candidates," *The Wall Street Journal*.]

elegiac

of or relating to sorrow or mourning; having a sorrowful or melancholy air; usually describes a piece of verse or prose. Noun is *elegy*. "While he spoke one sentence, sadness at the thought of Christine seemed to grip his tongue at the root and reduce him to an elegiac silence..." [Kingsley Amis, *Lucky Jim*.]

prefect

an administrative officer, especially one high up; president, chief officer, head. Commonly used in the plural, as in "religious prefects."

gesticulate

to gesture in an excited and animated way. "And the sonorous souls of Russian verbs lend a meaning to the wild gesticulation of trees or to some discarded newspaper sliding and pausing...along an endless wind-swept embankment." [Vladimir Nabokov, "That in Aleppo Once..."] "The pilgrims could be seen in knots, gesticulating, discussing. [Joseph Conrad, *Heart of Darkness*.]

seditious

tending to excite to rebellion or insurrection against the state (i.e., tending to promote sedition). Seditious speech is not protected by the first amendment, but it may be reported with impunity.

inexorable

relentless; not to be convinced otherwise or reasoned away. "So there she sat, her eyes now upon that inexorable blank sheet that lay before her, waiting, and now turned with vacant hopelessness upon the sundry objects in the room." [Owen Wister, *The Virginian*.]

altercation

a severe quarrel in words. This is generally much more severe than a mere argument, which may be simply a reasoned and orderly debate between lovers of logical thought. An altercation connotes zealous will between its contestants. Newspapers are beginning to use this as a synonym for "ruckus," which is rather more violent that wordy.

inscrutable

hard to understand or penetrate; mysterious. "It came at the end of his speeches, like a seal applied on the words, to make the meaning of the commonest phrase appear absolutely inscrutable." [Joseph Conrad, *Heart of Darkness*.]

denigrate

literally, to blacken, or to defame or sully; to attack a reputation. We may berate or deride somebody, and this action might have the effect of denigrating him. See *derisory*.

propitiate

to appease, or to bring about a favorable outcome; pacify. Noun is "propitiation." Adjective is "propitious." "He had learnt...how to predict Reinecke's shifting moods, how to propitiate his wrath..." [Patrick O'Brian, *Richard Temple*]

platitude

empty, banal, trite phrases with little meaning (e.g., "marching arm-in-arm to a brighter tomorrow"). "We asked the candidate what he intended to do, and all he gave us was platitudes."

derisory

expressing derision: tending to mock, or show scorn and contempt: derisive.

peremptory
    putting an end to a discussion or action. Not to be confused with *preemptive* (see below) but sadly often is, and vice versa. "The chairman lifted a peremptory hand, and the debate ceased."

preempt
    to sieze or purchase in a manner that prevents another party's doing the same; to take for oneself. Commonly used in the press to mean taking away power or capability; military people talk of pre-emptive strikes to reduce the abilities of an enemy before he has shown a determination to use them. *Co-opt* is often used as a synonym. *Preemtive* is the adjective—not to be confused with *peremptory*. "Just prior to the start of the war, the President authorized preemptive air strikes that holed Iraqi airfields, leaving Saddam's planes intact but utterly useless."

polemicize
    to initiate, or continue, a debate, dispute, or controversy; to deliver an argument. See *polemic*.

profundity
    deepness of intellect, feeling, or meaning.

adroit
    capable of completing tasks with apparent ease and skilful, adept effectiveness: deft. "But there is a mystery to Jeeves—the evident incongruity of this adroit and learned schemer working for an ass like Bertie." [Alexander Cockburn in an introduction to P.G. Wodehouse's *The Code of the Woosters*.]

percipient

capable of perception (in a clinical sense), or perceiving quickly or well. See *perspicacious*.

effete

worn out, no longer having vitality, no longer fertile; sometimes used in place of "effeminate." This word was brought into popular usage by Nixon's vice president Spiro Agnew, who in the late 1960s referred to some spear-throwing journalists as "an effete corps of impudent snobs." "That both Edwards and Obama are hamstrung by effete professional-class gender etiquette was suggested by the way that Dennis Kucinich...has been able to shatter the debate decorum with exhilarating bursts of derisive rhetoric." [Camille Paglia, "Don't Run Al. Don't!" in *Salon.com*.]

trite

becoming meaningless or powerless through repetition. "OK, OK, spare me the trite criticisms and tell what is really wrong with me."

vilify

to make vile or base through criticism or denouncement; to degrade; to intensely criticize, attempt to publicly degrade or defame. Compare to *revile, repudiate, denigrate*. "As a strategy, the Democrats have succeeded in vilifying each Republican Speaker and Vice President since the Nixon administration, going so far as to conduct weekly approval-rating polls for the Republican Speakers like Gingrich (unheard of during Democrat control of the House)." [Jack Liquide, *The Mess*.]

umbrage

resentment; the state of having been slighted or offended. Almost always seen in the usage "to take umbrage," but refreshingly not always: "Imus, a 30-plus-year veteran of radio shock, seemed to underestimate the power of the modern umbrage-amplification machine." [James Poniewozik, "The Imus Fallout: Who Can Say What?" in *Time Magazine*.]

depredate

to plunder or ransack. Used more often as a noun (depredation). The depredation resulting from Sherman's march is reviled even by those ultimately liberated by the effort.

churlish

having a common, rustic, or average demeanor; boorish; vulgar. "Churlish knave" is a trite example.

obtain (as an intransitive verb, i.e. not the usual usage)

to be the case; to become accepted, to become the norm or the usual. "[This publication] had long been under the impression they were rather *good* friends, but suspects this will not obtain in the future." [Timothy Noah, "Hitchens vs. Blumenthal," in *Slate.com*, Feb. 1999.]

vitriolic

caustic (or acidic, too, in the common usage), especially in speech or writing; capable of corroding in the figurative sense; biting and/or vicious. Noun is *vitriol*. (Not to be confused with *vitreous*, as in "vitreous china," which is a chemical term describing a ceramic that has gone through a glassification process.) See *sardonic* and *mordant*. "Bill's proclamation, among the dinner guests, of his continuing faithfulness brought a vitriolic stare from the wife he had so many times adultered...and from a few other women as well."

verisimilitude

not truthfulness, but rather the appearance of truth. Not "his shifty eyes belied his verisimilitude," but "his earnest expression gave him verisimilitude that belied his perjuring ways."

salient

standing out, protruding, especially notable. "Salient feature" is a hackneyed usage.

culpable

deserving of blame for wrongness or unlawfulness; resulting in guilt. *Culpability* is the noun. "Culpable act" is a hackneyed usage.

exculpatory

tending to exonerate or to show innocence of a charge. "It seems...that the judge's exclusion of some of this exculpatory evidence was a payback for Libby's decision not to take the stand..." [Christopher Hitchens, "Free Scooter Libby," in *Slate.com*.]

coterie

a small, perhaps select, group of people aligned by some common interest and who tend to hang out with each other frequently. "These Hungarians were part of the Wodehouse coterie..." [Alexander Cockburn in an introduction to P.G. Wodehouse's *The Code of the Woosters*.]

hackneyed
    very commonplace—usually refers to a phrase or literary situation that is all too familiar because of over-use. "The phrase, 'hackneyed phrase,' is itself a hackneyed phrase."

cacophonous
    having disconnected, un-harmonic sounds; discordant. "To defer to the House of Representatives and let the bill be thrown together by cacophonous mob rule made the president seem passive and behind the curve." [Camille Paglia, "A Rocky First Few Weeks," *Salon.com*.]

inveigle
    to win over by coaxing, disingenuous flattery, or artful talk. Not to be confused with *inveigh*. "...in an attempt to inveigle me to lend him my Porsche."

inveigh
    to give vent to angry disapproval; protest vehemently: to rail. Usually used with "against." "No prime-time series has more ardently inveighed against the Bush administration." [Ken Tucker, "Boston Legal," *Entertainment Weekly*.]

antecedent
    going before or preceding. "Abstinence is the antecedent virtue to chastity."

nictitate
    to wink. A pretentious synonym and best avoided unless the pretension is expected or called for: " 'My, you use big words for such a little man,'

The Vocabulary 39

she said. He cocked an eyebrow. 'Nictitate when you say that,' he said, and he winked at her as he turned to leave."

touchstone

a thing or event that has established the standard of excellence of those that follow. "Its reputation has only grown, becoming a touchstone for artists like Devendra Banhart and Joanna Newsom." [Stewart Smith, "Cold Comfort," *TheList.co.uk* (speaking of Vashti Bunyan's album, "Just Another Diamond Day.")

ostentatious

making a display of one's wealth or achievement, especially in a vainglorious manner. "...no healthcare bill is worth the paper it's printed on when the authors ostentatiously exempt themselves from its rules." [Camille Paglia, "Pelosi's Victory for Women," *Salon.com*.]

gambol

to run and skip about in play.

entreaty

an earnest plea. "...regarding her own false arrogance in the pierglass as if it were proof against the old woman's entreaties..." [Cormac McCarthy, *Cities of the Plain*.]

quiddity

the essence of a thing—that which answers the question "Quid est?" ("what is it?"). Might be used formally, say, in a coffee-table treatise on the use of garlic in the cuisine of Provence.

quid pro quo

something exchanged for something of equal value (literally, this for that, or tit for tat). "Congressman Roberts acquiesced in his opposition to Schultz's bill—probably as a quid pro quo for Schultz's vote on the Baxter bill."

paroxysm

convulsions or fits, perhaps as a renewal of previous symptoms; an outburst. "So amnesiac have we become, indeed, that we fall into paroxysms of adulation for a ward-heeling Chicago politician who does not complete, let alone "transcend," the work of Dr. King…" [Christopher Hitchens, "Obama is no King," in *Slate.com*.]

mordant

biting, caustic, and/or wickedly sarcastic in style or manner. (Sometimes used erroneously in confusion with "moribund" (dying), but meaning nothing of the sort.) "Richard Pryor's comedy was mordant but sympathetic, Lenny Bruce's mordant but complaining."

sententious

terse and weighty in expression; tending to moralize in few words. Pithy. "The *Mod Squad's* trio of converted-hippy detectives took 'heavy' to a new level, with every sententious look and phrase dripping with their own unearned and gloomy righteousness."

acerbic

sour or bitter in presentation, tone, or character. "acerbic wit" is a hackneyed use. Compare with *sardonic*. Noun is *acerbity*.

whilom

adjective: former, once. "The whilom brunette made a winsome blonde." Compare with *erstwhile*.

erstwhile

adverb: formerly, previously, heretofore. Adjective: former, previous...synonym for *whilom*.

conniving

colluding or cooperating secretly in some wrongful deed; affecting an innocent or ignorant air while engaged in or aware of wrongdoing. A hackneyed usage is "...why you conniving, two-timing, son of a bitch!"

eschatological

or or relating to the end of the world, or of man's ultimate destiny. "The book of Revelations: an eschatological skeet, shot by committee and put back together by same." Too often used pretentiously in place of "scatological," which rather denotes a preoccupation with bowel traits.

apostolic

of or relating to apostles. "The gurus of the self-help movement collectively limn the apostolic legacy of Norman Vincent Peale's Positive Thinker."

afflatus

the imparting of knowledge or power by divine means; a creative impulse or revelation. "The pulling from the stone of Arthur's sword, Excalibur, was an afflatus that justified generation upon generation of hereditary rule."

prestidigitation

sleight of hand. Used almost exclusively in an awed voice. "Bill Clinton diverted attention away from Gennifer Flowers's bedroom activities and onto George Bush's throne-room inactivities; it was a prestidigitation worthy of the slyest of politicians, and accepted by the most cynical of voting populations."

imprecate

to call an evil or curse upon. An imprecation is a curse. Not to be confused with "implicate."

prest

a loan of money; also as an adjective to mean "ready" (as in "presto"). "A few prests from fellow barflies kept him in his cups until a new round of loan officers was seated."

picaresque

of or relating to clever rogues, rascals, or adventurers. "A picaresque gallery, lining an upstairs hallway wall, promised an enjoyable hour at Nora's arm, some rainy evening, to be spent in study of her ancestors." Not to be confused with "picturesque"; keep an ear on the nightly TV news and you will certainly hear the two confused before long.

importune

to pester by making demands upon; beg urgently. "...until the world, that jade, yielded at last to his importunings and he became very famous—almost omnipresent—in his homeland." [James Parker, "Brit Wit," *The Atlantic*.]

manna
> food divinely supplied—"manna from heaven" is probably redundant, but commonly encountered.

sophistry
> subtly deceptive reasoning or argument, that appears sound on the surface but is not. "Through relentless use of the *reductio ad absurdum*, Buckley exposed the sophistry of countless smug adversaries."

evanescent
> tending or likely to vanish like vapor. As a noun, "evanescence." See *ephemeral.* "At odd times—in passing through the perfumed wake of an old-fashioned lady, or hearing an echo of footfalls and laughter among wood-floored rooms—an evanescent image of her would pass across his consciousness like a suddenly perceived constellation: a pattern of stars, suddenly perceived, that drifts back as suddenly into incoherent points of light against a topless void."

alacrity
> a cheerful promptness, willingness, or readiness in response. "His alacrity degenerated to mere resignation in the absence of an audience."

perfunctory
> characterized by routine, by superficial, uninterested, or mechanical action with little thought or enthusiasm. "Perfunctory glance" is a hackneyed use. "He was fatalistic about the certainty of his being fired one day, and his shoddy work—perfunctory as a result of this belief—was to be the eventual cause of the dismissal!"

eschew

to avoid, shun, abstain from, or reject. "Eschew defalcation" (avoid embezzlement) was a common bumper sticker in the 1970s.

irascible

easily brought to anger. "Irascible old coot" is a hackneyed phrase.

coot

senile person, especially a male.

canonize

to declare to be a saint; to ratify or sanction. "The faintest hue of acknowledged guilt colored his eyes, leaving his canonized smile intact but somehow disconnected to his face."

efficacy (or efficacity)

effectiveness; ability to produce the desired consequence. This is somewhat pretentious—"effective" will do the job efficaciously. As many have noted, the key to being glib is to "never use a dollar word when a nickel word will do."

obsequious

showing oneself to be servile or compliant to another, especially in an attempt to ingratiate; fawning. See *sycophant*. "A president needs a staff that appears obsequious while nevertheless giving advice that is dead-nuts right."

halcyon
    peaceful and calm, tranquil; prosperous and carefree. "The afternoon is the halcyon, the calm coming between earnestness and drama." [Adam Hall, *The Quiller Memorandum*.]

polity
    the political entity of rule or government composed by a specific people, organization, or group. "...as though mass extermination were the ultimate purpose of the bombing campaign just as it was the purpose of the Nazi polity." [Agis Valiunas, "Fire from the Sky," *Commentary*.]

laconic
    spare by habit in the use of words. See *terse* (which usually describes the words themselves, rather than the speaker), *taciturn* (not inclined to speak), and *reticent* (disinclined to be wordy in a particular situation).

ephemeral
    lasting only a very short while. "He was merely a man of action on a local scale, and an ephemeral journalist." [Philip Terzian, "The Revolutionist," *Commentary*.]

leviathan
    a gigantic version of something that is usually found somewhat smaller. "On quadrangles across the country, collegians slammed into one another until the blood and spittle flew, and leviathan stadiums were built to accomodate the growing pastime." [Sally Jenkins, "The Team That Invented Football," *Sports Illustrated*.]

comportment

the way one carries oneself; bearing. Pretentious in just about every use. "I've always thought it best to be continually witnessed in the most dignified of comportments, so as to render suspect any testimony regarding my drink-related asininities."

asinine

silly or ass-like.

equipoise

a condition of balance or equilibrium. See *equanimity*, which is more often used in describing a mental state rather than a physical one.

torpor

a state of sluggish passiveness; lethargic apathy . "In the second half, when everyone was seated, she overplayed her hand and began to intrude and domineer; the men sank into passive torpor." [Camille Paglia, "Don't Run, Al. Don't!" in *Salon.com*.]

contiguity

proximity, closeness. "Contiguous" is the adjective, meaning "touching," as in the trite "contiguous 48 states" used so fondly by TV weathermen instead of the less pedantic "lower 48."

paean

a joyous song sung in tribute to another; used more often in the figurative sense in which it is not sung but rather spoken or written. "'You like me,' gushed Sally Field, in a paean to the legions of fans who made the ultimate sacrifice and dragged themselves to see her movie."

apposite

    very appropriate, relevant. Probably better used than the hackneyed and pompous "apropos" in formal text, and better left out of conversation because of its similar sound to "opposite."

iambic

    poetry term describing a word having an unstressed syllable followed by a stressed, as in "repress." Most often encountered in the phrase "iambic pentameter," describing a meter in verse. "Hudspeth seemed not to depart but to fade, as the iambic gallop of his horse became distant and commingled, in Marie's lonesome ears, with the throb of the night crickets."

pustulate

    covered with pustules, i.e. oozing sores or abscesses. Rhymes with "amulet." "Purulent" describes them when they are oozing. Probably encountered more often as a metaphor, to wit:

        "Dirt and water blend
        In pustulate brown blurp blurp—
        The mud bath speaking."

pundit

    a source of opinion. Nowadays almost exclusively considered to be a member of the news media.

disquisition

    a formal discourse on a particular subject. *Inquisition* denotes an inquiry before a jury. "He'd given a short disquisition on the history and architecture of the mission and those who heard it would not believe that he had never been there." [Cormac McCarthy, *Blood Meridian*.]

perdition

a condition of eternal damnation. Seems to be used a lot by preachers to pussyfoot around "hell." "A few days into Billy's stay with us, all present judged his destiny to lie somewhere between juvenile detention and perdition."

obdurate

hardened in outlook or temperament; unyielding; persistent in following the wrong course. "It would be a gross understatement to say that reality proved a more complex and obdurate substance than was dreamed of in Carter's philosophy." [Arthur Herman, "The Return of Carterism," *Commentary*.]

transmogrify

to change with an often unintended grotesque or humorous end result. "A small pimple on the end of Clinton's nose was transmogrified unwittingly, through some error in stage make-up, into the visual focus of his second state-of-the-union address."

apotheosis

elevation to divine status; a perfect example. Used interchangeable with "epitome." "Mesquite-cooked anything became the apotheosis of western yuppie cuisine, and if it was cooked on a commercial range in some bond trader's adobe kitchen—well, it became sublime."

adumbrate

to foreshadow. Pretentious in all but literary usage. "Whether intended by Faulkner or not, the murder of Joe Christmas' father by active malice, and his mother by passive malice, adumbrated the fatalism that marked Christmas' final hour."

blench

to recoil from. "Mary blenched as Luther hocked up a mighty wad and arced it percussively toward a distant spitoon."

scarify

to break up the surface of something (like skin). "The scarified surface of his leather jacket spoke either of disregard for a fine piece of clothing, or of recent encounters with the road surface."

excoriate

literally, to tear or abrade the skin off of something. More usually, to strongly denounce, curse, or censure. "Nixon was excoriated in his first Kennedy debate."

internecine

relating to arguments or contention within an organization. "Internecine squabbles," which is seen too often, is redundant. "Given the high rate of internecine departures from his school board, the superintendent would do well to either solve the underlying issues or to get out."

exigencies

those things in a situation or occasion that require attention. Usually used in the plural. In singular (exigency): urgency. As an adjective (exigent): requiring attention. "At stake are legal and policy questions...involving a clash between the exigencies of national security and the most cherished provisions of our civil and political order." [Gabriel Schoenfeld, "In the Matter of George W. Bush *v.* the Constitution," *Commentary.*]

scrofulous

of or pertaining to tainted morals; (as a medical term) having scrofula— little seen nowadays but common in, say, the eighteenth century. "By contemporary standards Liz and Richard were merely bad at hewing to their wedding vows, but their infidelities were so scrofulous to INS gatekeepers of the 'Camelot' era that Liz was denied entry into the U.S."

inhere

to be fundamentally and irremovably part of something larger; to be innate. "...her eyes came up in the dark water like some other self of wolf that did inhere in the earth or wait in every secret place..." [Cormac McCarth, *The Crossing.*]

jejune

childish or adolescent; dull and lacking nutrition, lacking spice or flavor. This word is so little-used in conversation that it raises eyebrows. "Stillman is a careful observer with an obvious love of language, and his wonderful, fresh cast handles the script with ease, conveying just the right measure of deadpan, jejune super-seriousness." [(no author listed), TV-Guide.com, review of film *Metropolitan.*]

apprise

    to tell; to notify, to bring up to date. Not to be confused with *apprize* (to prize or to highly value) or *appraise*. "The boss apprised us of the new quotas."

somnambulant

    in a state of sleep while walking. "Since he became famous he has become infamous as well for a long string of phoned-in, somnambulant screen cameos."

indefatigable

    not easily tired; incapable of being brought to fatigue: untiring.

amenable

    answerable to authority; obedient to law or judgment.

officious

    meddlesome; excessively eager to offer unsolicited advice.

precipitous

    tending to rash, abrupt, hasty, headlong action; cliff-like, dangerous.

nexus

    a link in time or circumstance, or a set of things bound by a common link. (Probably pretentious except in learned compositions.) "Trash culture, establishment art, and a reverence for Roseanne Barr—their nexus is the acceptance and institutionalization of low-mindedness."

desultory

without plan or purpose. "The bulk of Samuel Johnson's formal education was a desultory romp—guided only by an exploding range of interest—through the library of a solicitous neighbor."

apogee

the highest point in a trajectory or path. Often used metaphorically: "As a reliable correspondent, I reached my apogee when I was most destitute and least capable of editing my thoughts." See *nadir, perigee*.

ascribe

to attribute to a specific cause or precursor or source. Noun is *ascription*.

dun

to demand upon for payment in an unusually or painfully persistent way. Usually seen as "dunning" or "dunned." "Nobody goes to that bar any more: it's always too crowded, and the bartenders dun you for your old tabs."

exiguous

meager in amount. "Dating for me was always a balancing act between passion for my girlfriend on the one hand, and on the other hand my passion for the exiguous reserve of cash that lay at the foundation of my inclination to pick up the tab."

apostasy

the renouncing of a faith; defection. As a noun (one who has left the faith) and adjective, "apostate." "To the other villagers, the boy's apostasy lay more in his words than in his thoughts, for indeeed none of them thought the emperor was clothed either."

rive

to tear open, to rip open, to rend, to cleave. Seen most often in the passive voice. "When men hear it they fall to their knees and their souls are riven…" [Cormac McCarthy, *The Crossing*.]

peregrine

tending to wander; as a noun, "peregrinations" (wanderings). Rhymes with "paraffin," sort of. "Given Liz's peregrine devotion to the ideal of romantic love, her life-long attachment to Richard Burton was out of character—but then she was great at acting."

profligate

recklessly wasteful and excessive, especially with money.

perforce

due to force of circumstance or necessity. "…through which the contemporary ironist must…perforce tiptoe on eggshells." [Mark Steyn, "The Hunting of the Denby, *Commentary*.]

recriminations

counter-charges against an accuser, made in an attempt to gain the offense. "In Whitewater, as in Watergate, the executive embraced recriminations against the press just as a drowning man might embrace a rotting log."

reprehensible

capable of or deserving of being censured or vilified. The distinction between this and its opposite, "irreprehensible," which is chiefly a legal term, is being blurred by the latter's misuse as a pejorative adjective. It is not uncommon to see somebody on TV saying, "the defendant's behavior was simply irreprehensible." (Talk about damning by faint praise...)

arcane

understood by a few who are in obscure professions or pursuits. Noun is *arcana*. "Before she found the Mickey Mantle rookie card, her obsession with low-end estate sales was written off by her friends as a nostalgic passion for arcane odd lots."

factitious

not formed by nature nor arising naturally; made up or constructed. "Does Hillary Clinton have a stable or coherent sense of self... or is everything factitious, mimed and scripted?" [Camille Paglia, "Hillary vs. Obama: It's a Drawl!", in *Salon.com*.]

incipient

commencing, beginning, barely formed; see *inchoate*, below. "Her incipient womanhood struggled for expression beneath the baggy jeans and XXL T-shirt."

inchoate

in a very early stage, perhaps imperfectly formed; difficult to perceive because of this. "An inchoate taste for Manhattans might have explained the way he awoke that morning: face down on the kitchen table, beside an empty pint bottle of sweet Vermouth and the bottom half of his father's new bottle of Jim Beam."

imminent

just about to happen; on its way. Impending. "...an imminent storm."

innocuous

seemingly harmless, not likely to offend or have a negative effect. "Thus her relationship with Herschel ended—not with a bang, but with an innocuous wimp."

moiety

a part of something larger; half of something, but perhaps with indistinct boundaries.

insouciant

nonchalant, blithely unconcerned, light-hearted. Noun is *insouciance*. "Blake's insouciant references to Camille's 'loving husband' were really a ploy to assess the strength of her marriage—and by extension, her willingness to fool around."

petulant

insolent, rude, or ill-tempered in speech or behavior; unreasonably so. "To paraphrase Thurber, their union was indeed blessed with issue: two petulant, whining, and clinging brats whose only saving graces were their mother's bone structure and their father's (with any luck heritable) history of outgrowing the bad habits of his youth."

punctilious
>strictly attentive to every detail.

insentient
>lacking in irritability, or lacking in senses and perception: unconscious. "Bill had been so excitable in the late afternoon, but his brief, though apparently active, turn at the bar had transformed him into an insencient bean bag."

odorous
>having a distinctive odor (implies neither good (*fragrant*) nor bad (*malodorous*)!).

insipid
>lacking in flavor, or those qualities that excite and challenge: dull. See *innocuous*. "The wine: piquant; the surroundings: exotic; the company: insipid. The evening: on balance, about a half-bottle to the positive."

trepidation
>nervous apprehension or dread; fear. "Reinforcing such trepidations among officials up and down the line was a 'swarm of lawyers...'" [Gabriel Schoenfeld, "In the Matter of George W. Bush *v.* the Constitution," *Commentary*.]

jaundiced
>predisposed to be skeptical and soured in outlook and perception, this due principally to envy or jealousy. "Looked upon it with a jaundiced eye" is a hackneyed but nevertheless apt usage.

phlegmatic

slow, stolid, imperturbable, unemotional—or suggestive of such a temperament. "...an enterprise that made him gasp and brought up blisters on his hand, but which was apparently not enough to keep him as well-balanced and phlegmatic as an ox." [Patrick O'Brian, *Richard Temple*.]

badinage

playful, witty banter. "...a person...who would talk pleasantly without the eternal facetious badinage of most of his acquaintance..." [Patrick O'Brian, *Richard Temple*.]

trenchant

forceful, vigorous, incisive: keenly effective. "His eyes, of the usual blue, were perhaps remarkably cold, and he certainly could make his glance fall on one as trenchant and heavy as an axe." [Joseph Conrad, *Heart of Darkness*.]

restive

disobedient; restless, agitated, discontent. "...signs of a political leadership that has run out of ideas and can now only futilely demand obedience from an increasingly restive citizenry." [Gordon G. Chang, "The End of the Chinese Miracle?" in *Commentary*.]

truculent

in the habit of fighting; combative, pugnacious; bitterly fierce. "...a chronicler of the truculent way of the trading pits, and possibly the definitive opposite of the Aquarian spirit." [Thomas Frank, "Dissent Commodified," Wall Street Journal.]

reproach

scolding criticism. ("Beyond reproach" is a hackneyed usage.)

taciturn

not inclined to speak; not wordy by nature. "A taciturn fellow: normally quiet, and above normal in restraint." Compare to *reticent*, which is the situational version of this.

untrammeled

unrestrained; without set limits. "The government in Ankara, which evidently believes that all European governments are as untrammeled as itself, brusquely insists that Denmark do what it would do and simply shut the transmitter down." [Christopher Hitchens, "Ankara Shows its Hand," *Slate.com*.]

decimate

original meaning: to destroy a tenth of something, like a population or army. Contemporary meaning: to utterly destroy! As Kingsley Amis has noted in *The King's English*, the establishment of two opposite meanings for this word has rendered it unusable, lamentably.

tacit

unspoken but understood nonetheless. "Tacit agreement" is a hackneyed usage. "They silently broke camp in a tacit understanding of the rigors that lay ahead of them."

hortatory

in an urging or commanding manner; intended to exhort. "Each rule or principal is followed by a short hortatory essay, and usually the exhortation is followed by…" [E.B. White, in his introduction to his and William Strunk, Jr.'s, *The Elements of Style.*]

chauvinist

one who is over-zealous in supporting a cause. (This does not have anything to do with anti-feminism; its original association with opposition to feminism was in the phrase "male chauvinist," i.e. championing the male over the female.)

contumely

a contempt borne of arrogance and conceit. "…Bush, a man who has demonstrated an unfailingly courageous willingness to endure vilification and contumely in setting his face against it." [Norman Podhoretz, "The Case for Bombing Iran," *Commentary.*]

supercilious

exhibiting a disdain for that which is thought to be beneath one. "His little eyes glittered like mica discs—with curiosity—though he tried to keep up a bit of superciliousness." [Joseph Conrad, *Heart of Darkness.*]

renascence

a revival or rebirth, especially cultural: renaissance. "Forty years after the sixties, we have seen in the grunge-rock movement a sudden renascence of the pseudo-deep, murky, and pretentious song lyrics that so effectively duped the fans of earlier alternative-rock groups like Crosby Stills & Nash and Steppenwolf."

banal
    drearily boring, commonplace, featureless, harmless. "A magic place-name has been pronounced, one that exorcises all the banality and evil of the surrounding circumstances." [Christopher Hitchens, "The Grub Street Years," *The Guardian (UK)*.]

temporize
    to evade and give excuses, as a means of gaining time. "…the temporizing Union generals such as George McClellan would be fired by an impatient Lincoln…" [Christopher Hitchens, "The Grub Street Years," *The Guardian (UK)*.]

serried
    jumbled together in rows. "In the shimmering distance, trees and jacales stood along the slender bights of greenland pale and serried and half fugitive in the clear morning air." [Cormac McCarthy, *All the Pretty Horses*.]

effulgence
    a striking radiance, brilliant shine. "The sky was lit here and there by the effulgence of some marshalling yard or night-working factory south of the river…" [Patrick O'Brian, *Richard Temple*.]

refulgence
    resplendence; glitter. Like *effulgence* but with richness.

bathos
    a transition in style or concept from the sublime to the commonplace or prosaic—often with ludicrous effect. "Is there a better example of bathos

than West Virginia's having changed its advertising tag-line from 'Almost Heaven' to 'Open for Business'?" [Note that we are almost inclined to say "that's pathetic!" when confronted with this example—but it's not really pathos we observe, but rather bathos!]

palaver

small and often mindless talk. "The air in the reception room was layered with the easy palaver of comfortable folks halfway through their first drinks."

turbid

difficult to see through, cloudy, opaque with suspended particles. "Turbid waters" is a hackneyed usage.

replete

filled or full, especially to abundance. Commonly used "replete with..." "The room was replete with stuffy people and their banal conversations—at least, that's how the most boring among them viewed it."

allay

to make calm, to alleviate, to lessen. "To allay one's fear" is a hackneyed usage.

pallid

lacking in color or interest. *Pallor* is the noun. "Pallid complexion" is a hackneyed usage. "...one live, drunken soldier, tremendously peripatetic and with only his pallor to connect him with death." [Vladimir Nabokov, "Time and Ebb."]

peripatetic

wandering, itinerant; walking about aimlessly.

loquacious

talkative, especially to excess.

abstemious

restrained, modest, or meager in one's appetite—for food, drink, or otherwise. "Like many politicians, Clinton was not nearly as abstemious in his ambitions as he was in his charity."

magniloquent

overly grand and lofty in speech: grandiloquent.

quiescent

calm, unmoving, quiet, unperturbed. "Her left arm—the one with the ring -- lazily draped over the low gunnel of the canoe, and her fingers spawned intermittent ripples that droned away from her in shimmering echelons atop the otherwise quiescent water."

obstreperous

defiant toward authority; rambunctious and noisy. "Sister Marcia would sound like a harmless old lady as she said, 'My, but you're obstreperous today,' but at the same time her strong hand was reaching for the yardstick."

prescient

having an accurate sense of what the future holds, especially in a specific instance.

lilt

a light, airy voice or song. "Lilting melody" is a hackneyed usage.

illimitude

the quality or state of being limitless or measureless. "...an illimitude of lenticular clouds stretched away from us, angling away from the dropping sun and bending over some distant hills."

virescence

the quality or state of becoming green.

pestiferous

infected with or breeding disease; deadly; annoying (like a pest...). "Sally and I were resigned to watching TV on the couch, at an arm's length from each other, since her pestiferous little brother had no intention of going to bed."

impute

to attribute, fault, or credit something wrongly or deviously.

rife

prevalent and widespread. (Note it takes a preposition, usually "with.") "The once-verdant pampas, now trampled, rutted, and sparse, was rife with the symptoms of overgrazing."

dyspeptic

gloomy and sullen. "A quick glance at the dyspeptic face of the judge was all I needed to predict the outcome of this trial."

verdure

the green of growing vegetation. (*Verdant* is the adjective.) "...the Colorado River Valley, whose verdure near Yuma was made all the more green by its contrast to the distant sand dunes."

raiment

clothing or garments. "...appeared in glorious and kingly raiment."

miscreant

a villain, a sinner; a doer of evil.

accede

to agree or give consent, on the insistence of others. "After weeks of vacillation in the face of continual cajoling and lobbying, the senator finally acceded and promised his vote."

veracity

the degree to which something is true or a person is truthful. "The commissioner dispatched Detective Jones to check the veracity of the informer's statements."

veracious

honest; believed to be or proven to be habitually true.

devolve

to pass on or to delegate; to be settled (as a task or duty) upon some other (lower) level of responsibility, as if flowing downhill. "As ever, what my boss leaves undone ultimately devolves to me."

The Vocabulary

remand
to send or order back. "Dad said 'no,' so I went to Mom instead—but she remanded my request to Dad."

reprove
to show disapproval; to rebuke.

flummox
to confuse or perplex. "I will admit, I was flummoxed by that last question."

curmudgeon
an ill-tempered person full of resentment and stubbornness. "One more ill look from him and I will be obliged to bludgeon the curmudgeon."

misogynous [also, **misogynistic**]
hating women; characterized by such. "…his misogynous rantings, whenever he was turned down."

apnea
a temporary cessation of breathing. "…in that first stunned, uncomprehending apnea after hearing the news…"

cretin
(commonly) a stupid, dull person. [Incredibly, this is a slang contraction of the Latin *christianus*, or "blessed person," used to mercifully denote, in olden times, that the mentally retarded are, after all, just human.]

insensate
    lacking sensation or awareness: foolish. Unfeeling, brutish.

philistine
    smug, ignorant, materialistic person who is indifferent to or disdainful of learning about arts and culture.

blandishment
    speech or action that tends to flatter, cajole, or wheedle. Used most often in the plural. Verb is *blandish*. "...immune to her blandishments but not to her beauty."

parse
    to break a statement or sentence down into its functional parts; to subject to detailed analysis. "The misstatement of politicians are parsed by their apologists—official and in the press—until they sound as innocous as their platforms."

extempory
    spoken, done, or composed with little or no preparation. Compare with *extemporaneous*.

extemporaneous
    spur-of-the-moment; prepared in advance (perhaps) but delivered without notes, as in a speech.

canon
    a law, rule, or code of law, especially of a church or of a discipline, made by authority thereof; an accepted or established rule; the body of work by

a writer, or of a genre, that are considered authentic. "...the canonical equations of thermodynamics." "...the Western Literature canon..."

iniquity

gross immorality or injustice: wickedness; a departure from just dealings. Adjective is *iniquitous*.

jeremiad

a piece of writing or speech that expresses a bitter lament or denunciation; a tirade of lament.

gadfly

a person who annoys or stirs one from lethargy.

aver

to verify or prove to be true. "...he will aver to my statement." Not to be confused with *avert*.

de jure

by right. Not to be confused with *de jour* (of the day).

de facto

actual (as opposed to de jure).

rubric

a classification, or categorization, under which an undertaking is done. "...a mass firing under the rubric of 'downsizing.'"

acuity

sharpness of perception or comprehension. "Her appreciation of my wit showed her to be a woman of great acuity."

redound

to have an effect, or to accrue: conduce. "Otherwise, why would they overlook [the fact] that unchecked punitive measures on producers will ultimately redound to everyone's economic detriment, not just the producers? [David Limbaugh, "Hillary's Quick Trigger Finger," *World Net Daily*.]

pantheon

a temple dedicated to all the gods (as opposed to one.) "The first step in his elevation to the pantheon came with the publication in 1967 of *Hitchcock/Truffaut*..." [Terry Teachout, "The Trouble with Alfred Hitchcock," *Commentary*.]

sagacious

wise; keen in perception, or expressing such. "...her sagacious assessment of my grim prospects."

iconography

visual representation of thought by pictures or symbols: especially, hackneyed meaning attached to an object. "Stalin's abject pragmatism was at odds with the pure iconography of the hammer and sickle."

patois

illiterate or provincial speech; jargon. "...immersed in the numbing, white-noise patois that formed the lingua franca of the market."

delusive

deceptive, causing one to be deluded.

litany

a repetitive or resonant chant or recital. "The judge read out a litany of the crimes he
been charged with."

pander

to attempt to gratify or aid in gratifying another's desires, especially unwholesome ones; to cater to or exploit weaknesses.

venial

forgivable, pardonable, easily excused. Not to be confused with *venal*, which is nearly the opposite! "...a venial offense, to be fixed with a broom and dustpan and not a noose."

venal

capable of being bought or corrupted; corrupt. "Venal officials, shaking hands with palms upturned."

gabble

to talk incoherently, talk aimlessly, talk fast or foolishly: jabber.

traduce

to betray, humiliate, defame, or malign through falsehoods. "As the Czech President, Vaclav Klaus, an economist, anti-totalitarian and climate change skeptic, prepares to take up the rotating presidency of the European Union next year, climate alarmists are doing their best to traduce him." [Miranda Divine, "Beware the Church of Climate Alarm," *Sydney Morning Herald.*]

dulcet

sweet-sounding, melodious. "...the dulcet lilt of her voice as she unabashedly sang to herself."

canard

a deliberately false or misleading story; one that is popularly told but commonly known to be false. "What flatulent canards mainstream feminism used to traffic in!" [Camille Paglia, "Obama's Hit—and Big Miss," *Salon.com.*]

seminal

having the claim to being the original, or the source. "His was the seminal work on the heritability of diabetes."

oxymoron

a combination of contradictory words, often used rhetorically e.g. "a dreary brilliance" or "elegant squalor" or "a healthy case of the flu." "Military intelligence" is offered up by fuzzy thinkers as an example of this.

inure (also enure)

to accustom or harden to something unpleasant. "...inured to the rigors of hard study."

torpid

> lazed; deprived of motion; seemingly insensate or numb; lethargic. "...while downstairs their kids, not knowing each other and not particularly wanting to, lay recumbent and torpid in front of the television."

mendacious

> given to deception or falsehood: lying.

vitiate

> to contaminate, pollute; to debase or pervert; to lessen the value of. "There was no time to do anything at all except adopt the attitude of one waiting outside a bathroom, a stratagem vitiated to some extent by the raincoat he still wore." [Kingsley Amis, *Lucky Jim*.]

blithesome

> cheerful, gay and merry, unmindful of any bad or care, especially for the moment ("a blithesome gathering"); *blithe* means gay and merry and unseeing, by nature.

blithe

> cheerful, lighthearted, carefree by nature.

gentry

> the well-born or ruling class, though not of the nobility. "The landed gentry" is a hackneyed usage.

coercion

> act of restraint or domination by nullifying an individual's will.

harangue

a ranting, pompous, bombastic, or vigorously didactic address. "Gore proved, in every smug harangue, that he knew as little about the science of climate as he did about the economics of the energy business."

indissoluble

incapable of being dismantled, dissolved, ended. "Our indissoluble friendship…"

vituperative

ill-intentioned, full of abusive censure and bitterness. "Vituperative attacks" is trite. "Vituperation" is the noun. "The man gave us a vituperative account of his parents' attempts at raising him well, and to see his ungrateful telling of it was to believe his parents' effort to have been futile."

obtrude

to impose one's ideas or self upon others, or to be thrust uninvited into something. "But for a moment into his grandiloquent dream obtruded the memory of long rows of malicious adolescent faces…" [Graham Greene, *The Orient Express*.]

expiate

to atone for, to pay a penalty or reparations for. "I hope this little gift expiates my lateness."

avatar

the incarnation or embodiment of something, especially of a concept, quality, or philosophy ("an avatar of virtue"); one phase of a continuing entity. "The players and accusers were viewed less as individuals than as avatars of competing political and cultural agendas." [Justin Pope (Associated Press), in *The Philadelphia Inquirer*.] "...through which she advanced in identical and anonymous and deliberate wagons as though through a succession of creakwheeled and limpeared avatars like something moving forever and without progress..." [William Faulkner, *Light in August*.]

craven

characterized by fear; defeated or vanquished (in Britain, one cries "craven" instead of "uncle"); lacking courage.

athwart

across, in opposition to; from side to side. "She lay athwart the couch, remote control in hand."

trice

a brief space of time , and instant ("in a trice"); to tie down or secure.

opine

to give an opinion, especially in a annunciatory way.

tendentious

having a strong and inherent point of view; partisan. "The stipulations that follow this turgid preamble are even more tendentious and become more so as the resolution unfolds." [Christopher Hitchens, "Don't Say a Word," *Slate.com*.]

inimical
    hostile or injurious in effect, especially to an idea or concept; having the temperament or quality of an enemy. "But Jeeves will not take orders inimical to his safety and Bertie would not dream of clinching a proposal with a command." [Alexander Cockburn in an introduction to P.G. Wodehouse's *The Code of the Woosters*.]

sang-froid
    calmness and assuredness under stress or strain. "Bond, shackled and tied, contemplated both the lit fuse and the swaying cobra with equal sang-froid."

naif
    an uncritical, guileless, innocent, natural person. "Among the fresh hires in the training class, the young engineers were the naifs, with their sweet expectations that the jobs that lay ahead consisted of nothing that couldn't be worked out on a calculator."

prodigal
    abundantly wasteful. This does not mean "wandering," although many use it in that sense, presumably in misinterpretation of the Bible story about the prodigal son—who was not only wasteful but a wanderer as well. "The in-your-face presence of reams of packaged-up, fresh paper, stacked so high near the printer that it resembled some sort of Guttenberg bunker, seemed an encouragement for us to print whatever and however much we prodigally wanted—trees be damned!"

remonstrate

to plead one's case in protest or objection. "Louise again asked Trace to interfere, but she could see by Cash's face that he was way beyond remonstrating with." [John Cheever, "O Youth and Beauty!"]

bellicose

eager for a fight. "...when the bellicose drunk, the crapshooter, the pianist, and the woman faced with the expiration of her hopes had all expressed themselves..." [John Cheever, "O Youth and Beauty!"]

sonorous

sounding deep and resonant. "With the sonorous words of the Our Father in a darkened room the children's day was over, but the day was far from over for Louise Bentley." [John Cheever, "O Youth and Beauty!"]

virulent

poisonous, deadly, capable of producing great harm. "...we seem on the brink not of popular revolution but of a malign mutation of the Islamic republic into something even more virulent and destabilizing." [Mark Steyn, "Iran and US," *steynonline.com*.]

assuage

to make less severe or intense, especially in the eyes of the one doing the assuaging. To "assuage my guilt" is a hackneyed usage, i.e. "After I broke it off with her, I sent her some roses to assuage my guilt."

disparate

fundamentally unequal or different. "The tracks shining in the wet lamplight ran on...to where they lay embedded in the bridge like great surgical clamps binding those disparate and fragile worlds..." [Cormac McCarthy, *Cities of the Plain*.]

complacent

content and self-satisfied, unconcerned. Noun is *complacence*. See also *complaisant*. "Nobody had ever fallen from the platform, so I guess their complacence was rational—if not understandable—when the express train blasted past their jaded gazes at 80 mph."

jaded

dulled and worn, this due to wearying experience or over-indulgence; dissipated.

blase

unimpressed by much, as if from over-exposure to worldly things.

complaisant

willing to be led; amiable, wanting to please. Like *complacent* but without the self-pleased component.

remunerate

to pay; to pay back; to compensate by paying money to. Noun is *remuneration*.

dissolute
    lacking in moral restraint or judgment in personal behavior; engaging in vices.

enervate
    to weaken or cause to have less vitality.

sycophant
    a self-serving flatterer of people of influence. "If I must have servants, make them givers of luxury. If I must have subjects, make them sycophants—they must give me majesty."

acquiescent
    tending to comply or accept without comment. Verb is *acquiesce*. "She was acquiescent, but according to the rules of our college I couldn't press on unless she explicitly gave me permission in the form of a complete statement. So I never got past first base, because she was taught by her mother never to talk about sex."

factious
    tending to break into factions, or tending to create factions or dissent; of or relating to factions. "I think the un-criticized—nay, applauded—formation of caucuses in the Senate has led to a broader atmosphere of factious self-interest there."

peroration
    the final summing-up at the end of a speech or discussion. Verb is "perorate," best left to the pompous. "His peroration died like a half-remembered punch line."

augur
    to foretell or predict. Usually used with the adverb "well." "His high income augurs well for a quick marriage to a trophy wife." Not to be confused with *auger*, which is a type of drill or screwshaft.

presage
    As a verb: to warn in advance or portend; foreshadow; accent on first syllable. As a noun, an omen or sign of things to come, and rhymes with sausage, sort of. "Ever the optimist, Blake interpreted her raised middle finger as a presage of intimacies."

deign
    to stoop or condescend, in acknowledging. "She affected to take little notice of us, but she deigned to nod at me as she turned for the punchbowl."

impone
    to stake or wager. Probably pedantic in most usages. "Jake imponed her to an evening's libations, on the mistaken bet that later she would be either grateful, or powerless." Not to be confused with *impugn*.

invective
    abusive, attacking, denouncing language.

succinct
    having expression in just a few words; concise, terse.

terse
    brief and to the point, especially as a rule or habit.

impugn

to assail or attack as questionable; to invalidate or charge as false. "Impugn the motives" is a hackneyed use. "Later in his secon term, the President's evocations of a beleaguered middles class were impugned as a cynical bid for the appearance of empathy for the little people."

hubris

in Greek mythology, the fatal mistake of challenging the gods. In real life: excessive pride, a presumption of position or privilege, or arrogance. "Franken often refers to himself as a 'satirist,' which is a piece of hubris that comes to him too glibly and naturally." [Christopher Hitchens, "Cheap Laughs," *The Atlantic*.]

tumescent

swollen, especially in the process of becoming swollen. "...the tongue tumescent and aching for the orgasm of speech..." [Adam Hall, *The Quiller Memorandum*.]

chauvinism

extreme or militant advocacy and glorification of one's country; fanatical belief in the superiority of one's kind. "Male chauvinism" is a contemporary usage, but the word in no way denotes this particular brand of chauvinism.

enmity

ingrained hatred, especially mutual. "In *Who's Afraid of Virginia Woolf* we eavesdrop on a mutual enmity, born of long-suppressed resentment and brought to maturity by close quarters."

animus
>a mood of animosity and antagonism that colors one's actions. "Her smile showed the strain of a long contest between the weight of animus and the bouying memory of genuine pleasures."

deus ex machina
>an improbable event that saves the day, perceived as the "hand of God" reaching down and setting things to right. "[While] Wooster...is a character...Jeeves, to the end of his days, remains a type—the *deus ex machina* who saves the day when all seems lost, the great artificer who ties up the loose ends and who rescues Bertie from the consequences of his repeated follies." [Alexander Cockburn in an introduction to P.G. Wodehouse's *The Code of the Woosters*.]

artificer
>a skilled craftsman; one who contrives something.

recondite
>not easily seen (i.e., understood); cloaked or hidden. "The hints of recondite habits remained in his lodgings long after the Ripper had fled them."

cogent
>convincing by appeal to the powers of reason or intellect.

probity
>integrity complete and confirmed (by others); uprightness.

obfuscate

to make darkened or confused, less understandable. Noun is *obfuscation*. "Hillary's health-care-reform task force obfuscated the process to the point where nobody but the inner circle knew its direction; I will never think of Madam Defarge again as anything but a middle-aged blonde."

rencounter

a brief fight or confrontation.

feckless

ineffective, without consequence; irresponsible. "Could public opinion of our feckless Congress sink any lower? You betcha!" [Camille Paglia, "A Rocky First Few Weeks," *Salon.com*.]

vet

to subject to a thorough appraisal or examination. "In consideration of the torturous vetting to which my wife would certainly put my evening's wanderings, I made my ascent of the stairs as ghost-like as drunkenly possible."

cloy

to cause distaste for something that was originally pleasant. "...Halloween children, their tastes cloyed by the indulgence of too much chocolate."

entail

imposing as a necessary accompaniment or consequence. "...the study of physics entails a study of calculus."

pedantic
>making a show of knowledge or learning, especially in a narrow or niggling way. "'I had just returned from Brussels—that's the largest city in Belgium,' he added, pedantically."

pedagogic
>tending to teach (whether welcome or not...); of or relating to teaching or instruction.

dilettante
>one who merely dabbles in something, usually an art or scholarly pursuit. "In love she was an expert, but she was a dilettante in virtue."

chattel
>one' peronal property, but that which is movable—i.e., not real estate. "In those faces that shall now be forever nameless among their outworn chattels..." [Cormac McCarthy, *The Crossing*.]

vicarious
>imagined or felt only through the experience of others; performed or implied by a proxy. "In the novel itself, one can often detect strong hints of a vicarious approval of what is ostensibly being satirized." [Christopher Hitchens, in a forward to Aldous Huxley's *Brave New World*.]

ingenuous
>showing innocent openness, lack of scheming; artless. "I think her interest in him was ingenuous at first, but as her estimation of his wealth grew, so did her guile."

beset
    persistently to weigh down, bedevil, harass, and/or vex; to attack. "At the hospital [David Brudnoy] came to terms with the besetting realities of his situation." [William F. Buckley, "Life is Not a Rehearsal: A Review," in *National Review*, Jan. 27, 1997.]

oeuvre
    the total output of an artist's life. "Indeed, one might say [of Kingsley Amis's works] that the diminishing returns of the avid sexual life are a leitmotif in the entire oeuvre." [Christopher Hitchens, "One Fraught Englishman," *The Atlantic*.]

leitmotif
    a musical theme or melody associated (in a work, such as a movie or opera) with a specific character; a recurring theme.

disingenuous
    not ingenuous; acting in a way that suggests one doesn't know facts that are actually known; crafty.

juggernaut
    an overwhelming thing that crushes others in its path. "...Microsoft, the software juggernaut."

lexicon
    a dictionary; a set of words used in a particular field or occupation.

engender

to cause to exist or develop. "A sudden and unprovoked thought of that furry part between a squirrel's ears popped into my head, and engendered a sort of giggle in my muscles—I couldn't even hang on, much less do a pullup; it was a bad start to boot camp."

predilection

a prior slant in favor of something. "The serving of tea—even when I have asked for it—always reminds me of my predilection for coffee."

ablution

an act of cleansing or washing one's body parts, usually as part of a ritual. More often seen in the plural. "Sex to me is holy, and prefatory ablutions in the ol' hot tub are a big part of the liturgy."

impunity

freedom from the expectation of punishment or retribution. "I was the smallest kid on the bus for many years, and various indignities were inflicted upon me with impunity by the big dumb goofs and the big smart goofs alike."

immure

to confine as if behind walls; to entomb. Not to be confused with *inure*. "The punishment would be more than she could bear: her hair would be cut off and she would be immured forever behind a convent wall." [Virginia Cowles, *The Romanovs*.]

vehement

expressed forcefully, or showing vigorous, emotional conviction. Noun is *vehemence*. "...a vehement protest against an egregious injustice." "...Miss Cutler vehemently dressed as a bridesmaid in the fashions of the First World War." [Kingsley Amis, *Lucky Jim*.]

tableau

a setting or scene that is vividly recalled or described—perhaps incidental but nonetheless remembered. "Sometimes when I need to remember a list of things, I imagine a tableau in which they all somehow appear."

disconsolate

unable to be consoled or reassured. "Like Homer, [Wodehouse] knew that relaxation meant inattention, sleep, or disconsolate grumblings that bards are not what they used to be in the old days." [Alexander Cockburn in an introduction to P.G. Wodehouse's *The Code of the Woosters*.]

puissance

the display or possession of power or might. Adjective is *puissant*. The very sound of the word conveys the opposite connotation, *impuissance*. Best avoided in conversation.

sonority

resonance; the condition of being sonorous—having a rich sound. "Madeline's voice had that sultry sonority that young smokers will have, and the fact that someday it would be a fading rasp was lost, of course, on her and her suitors."

usurp

to seize and occupy unrightfully. "...usurp the throne."

morose

having a gloomy or melancholy disposition. Not to be confused with *mordant* (dead) or *moribund* (dying). "As a confirmed member of Generation X, his face advertised the morose fatalism—suitable for a CD cover—that was the banner of his ilk."

hoyden

a saucy, rowdy, carefree woman or girl. "Jane Fonda has married the California assemblyman, Tom Hayden, so here's a headline for you: 'Hayden Bags Hoyden.'"

bridle

to show angry resentment, especially as a response. "He bridled at the suggestion that his sport coat was outdated."

co-opt

to take or assume for one's use; to appropriate. "But, as in other parts of the globe, the disaffected have become co-opted into something bigger." [Mark Steyn, "Thais Undone," *National Review* in *SteynOnline*.]

provenance

origin or source. "The toilet seat was covered with a liquid of no uncertain provenance."

rancor

bitter, deep-seated ill will. *Rancorous* is the adjective. "After Streisand got the *Dolly* role, Channing's rancor should have been directed at the film's producers rather than its star, but it was easier for her to forgive stupidity than virtuosity."

auspicious

attended or accompanied by favorable circumstances. "…an auspicious occasion."

inveterate

long-established; firmly rooted; persisting in a habit. "…an inveterate bachelor."

anodyne

as a noun: that which sooths. As an adjective: something soothing or relaxing, or capable of that. "I have no doubt that the *Concert for Diana's* anodyne character contributed to the underwhelming response to Live Earth." [Matthew Moore, "Why Live Earth Was a Dead Loss," *Telegraph (UK)*.]

> "front porch anodyne
> ice, bronzed mint, silver chalice—
> a Jim Beam julep."

laudatory

expressing praise. "The speech was laudatory, though unenthusiastic."

rebuke
    (as a verb) to criticize or disapprove sharply. (As a noun) a sharp criticism. "I offered a helping hand, only to receive a rebuke for appearing to patronize."

meretricious
    attractive in the way a prostitute is; seductive but false. "President Kennedy was adept at co-opting intellectuals with a taste of the meretricious glitz of Camelot." (Holman Jenkins, "Madonna, Cindy, and George,", *Wall Street Journal*, Sept. 14, 1995.)

cant
    hypocritical language composed of platitudes, trite sentiments, and false piety, and intended to mask the guile of the speaker. "As it turned out, every hip review of *Piss Jesus* inadvertently explicated not the piece, but rather the shameful cant of the reviewer -- who in his rush to embrace the printed message beside the sculpture, gushed over a piece of found art that could have been reproduced by any drunk Philistine's mindlessly filling up a bedpan."

equable
    serene, marked by lack of extremes; uniform; steady. Not to be confused with "equitable." "In the sense that he appeared to be publicly equable and privately manic depressive, Nixon showed he was cast from the same mold as any other true politician."

ensconced
    settled comfortably or securely. "...ensconced in his big chair where nobody could budge him."

fetter (or **fetters**)

a rope or chain used to restrain or hold one down. See *enfetter* also, for the verb form.

obstreperous

clamorous and noisy; stubbornly boisterous; defiant. One seems to envision this word's being used by Tom Sawyer's aunt, and no others.

captious

(in argument) intended to confuse or entrap; (as a character trait) tending to complain about or point out small defects and faults. See *cavil, querulous, peevish.* "She recently had acquired a habit of captious criticisms—my rough hands, the way one of my eyelids opened wider than the other—which led me to suspect that her heart was no longer as much into romance as mine."

annunciatory

as if announcing.

affable

easy and pleasant, especially to those approaching anew. "I sought an affable face to ask about directions to the subway."

cavil

to raise trivial points in objection. "Clinton caviled when Wolf Blitzer asked him why he called a slowdown in the rate-of-increase in spending a 'cut': he said he only did it because Blitzer's colleagues started it." "Where others may have sought conciliation with the crown, or caviled at the prospect of armed confrontation with Britain, [Samuel] Adams saw the situation simply and clearly." [Philip Terzian, "The Revolutionist," *Commentary*.]

chasten

to take to task; to correct by rebuke—often administered by oneself as a result of new self-knowledge. "Anyone who has actually had to take responsibility for consequences by running any kind of enterprise—whether economic or academic, or even just managing a sports team—is likely at some point to be chastened by either the setbacks brought on by his own mistakes or by seeing his successes followed by negative consequences that he never anticipated." [Thomas Sowell, "Ego and Mouth," Townhall.com.]

expedient

(as an adjective) having the effect of speeding things up or making a task easier; benefitting only oneself; self-interested. (As a noun) something that is an end in itself, or that benefits some purpose. "He considered using soap as a pomatum, but decided against it, having in the past several times converted the short hairs at the sides and back of his head into the semblance of duck-plumage by this expedient." [Kingsley Amis, *Lucky Jim*.]

copse

a grouping or thicket of smaller trees or shrubs. "Beyond the low garden wall a path led to a copse of some small flowering trees, and its disappearance there held the promise of hidden meetings and whispers."

levity

excessive or inappropriate frivolity. "After Ron's funeral, once the President realized the camera had caught his moment of levity, he immediately bowed his head and wiped a tear."

sanguine

literally, blood-red. But usually: sturdy, hearty, optimistic, and confident, especially in one's expectations. "Those of us in the office were not especially sanguine about Gerald's prospects, especially after what he did in the punchbowl."

nebulous

cloud-like; vague (wispy), lacking form. "…a nebulous argument for election reform."

prevaricate

to avoid or evade the truth.

furtive

characterized by stealth and hidden motives. "Furtive glance" is a hackneyed usage.

"Dull, furtive windows in old tottering brick
Peered at me oddly as I hastened by."
(H.P. Lovecraft, "Fungi from Yuggoth.")

abject

hopelessly down in spirit or circumstance. "Today's 'abject poverty" is yesterday's 'scraping by.'"

abstruse
    difficult to understand; beyond the ken of ordinary understanding. "Dennis Miller's abstruse ramblings leave half his audience chuckling and the other half scratching heads."

abjure
    to reject, renounce under oath. "In world-wide forums Arafat has abjured terrorism, but the news hasn't yet reached his circle of close friends."

charlatan
    one making dishonest or fraudulent claims to specialized knowledge; a quack. "Einstein asserted that any scientist who could not explain his own subject to the satisfaction of a child was a charlatan."

caveat
    a warning or caution, especially one that qualifies a piece of advice or admonition. "Is the last line of our anthem a question, or a caveat: does the banner yet wave, or are we not the land of the free?"

imperium
    supreme power or authority; dominion. "...the surrender of imperium, in the belief that this act ultimately would extend his family's reign."

lurid
    sensational, shocking, stunning to one's comprehension. "...lurid images of mayhem and brutality."

append
   to add as a supplement or appendix.

sylvan
   of or relating to the woods or forest; made of forest materials like boughs and twigs.

perquisite
   a special privilege or benefit attached to an office or position. Nowadays abbreviated as "perk," alas.

reticulate
   resembling a net or network; like a net or a purse, with a cinch at top. (A *reticule* is a purse or handbag with a string closure.) "As the descended moon's brightness faded beyond the mountains, Orion gradually materialized, brightening and reticulate, atop a dark plume of low clouds."

dysgenic
   detrimental to the genes of one's offspring. "After typical swing through a small town, his dysgenic escapades left the beds of a few lonely maidens a little creakier."

shibboleth
   a test-case, a criterion for membership or standing in a group. "Even a basic feminist shibboleth like abortion rights became just another card for Pelosi to deal and swap." [Camille Paglia, "Pelosi's Victory for Women," *Salon.com*.]

adduce

to cite or refer to as evidence in support of an argument. "And the evidence adduced by the House of Commons must necessarily be considered by Scotland Yard..." [Christopher Hitchens, "The Galloway Papers," in *Slate.com*.]

gratuitous

unjustified, uncalled for; given without compensation. Usually used in pejoratively, as in "gratuitous violence, gratuitous praise, gratuitous advice."

obviate

to make unnecessary, especially logically. "I will adopt the boss's writing style in an attempt to obviate his editing me." Often seen, alas, in the redundant usage, "to obviate the need..."

casuistry

subtly deceptive verbiage, especially in its reasoning. "Nobody wants a dawning presidency addicted so soon to stonewalling, casuistry, and the Nixonian dark arts..." [Camille Paglia, "Obama's Early Stumbles," *Salon.com*.]

heterodox

reflecting unorthodox views or standards, especially religious. "Clutching his bible tightly, and high enough that it would appear in any camera shot of his face, the President walked a Sunday path that belied the heterodox philandering and untruths that lent character to his weekdays."

impudent
  having cheek or unwarranted boldness; offensively fresh in attitude.

epicure
  one who delights in and has a refined taste for food and drink, *Epicurean* is the adjective.

pernicious
  highly injurious or destructive, deadly, especially through deceit or corruption. "Pernicious rumors" is a hackneyed usage, although often accurate.

quintessence
  the purest, most refined, and central quality of a thing. "The quintessence of love is its survival past infatuation; reciprocation merely makes it sweet."

inane
  empty; having no substance; silly. "…went to them in search of deep pronouncements, but heard nothing but inane platitudes."

anomaly
  that which is misnamed—something that doesn't fit a pattern, or a syndrome, or the facts of a matter. "Anomalous" is the adjective. "Holmes's methodology could be summed up as a search for anomalies."

sacrosanct
  inviolable by its sacred status; used more in the secular sense. "The notion of succession by merit is sacrosanct to the great body of white-collar

workers, but not necessarily to their masters; something more indefinable is at work, and this worries the folks in Human Resources a lot."

tenable

capable of being rationally held or maintained. "Untenable position" is trite though often accurate. "Chamberlain's estimation of Hitler's trustworthiness, though untenable, must have been a great comfort to him."

conundrum

a question that has no verifiable or rational answer; an unsolvable problem. "Whether global warming is happening or not is a conundrum, but it is undeniable that the world's carbon is being oxidized at a greater rate than carbon dioxide is being fixed into hydrocarbons."

apostrophe

a digression during a speech or writing, usually by addressing somebody or something not present. "He suddenly looked to the ceiling and, in an apostrophe to his former wife, said, 'May you someday miss me!'"

hiatus

a break or interlude in an activity or pattern. "Brief hiatus" is trite. "During the hiatus in my studies afforded by this bout of hepatitis, it occurred to me that my talents lay more in the contemplation of beautiful things that in the design of door hinges."

misanthrope

one who hates or is contemptuous of other people. Not to by confused with a misogynist, who hates only half of other people. *Misanthropic* is

The Vocabulary

the adjective. "We tend to be misanthropic while driving to the liquor store, but we warm up rapidly once we are in front of the shelves."

reticent

not inclined to speak or object in a particular situation; also, reserved, unwilling. "Upon Bob's promotion, his coworkers were suddenly more reticent about his afternoon power naps."

redolent

emitting a strong fragrance. "...redolent with virtue, and stinking of hypocrisy"

antipathy

opposition in feeling, or in affection; repugnance. "Great deal of antipathy" is a trite usage. "Her antipathy for the rule of law was only exposed when she was caught at breaking one; otherwise she appeared to be a classic libertarian."

assiduous

diligent, constant, attentive to the task and its details. "...a man who, when he is being most assiduous in his work, is most dilatory within his family."

pervasive

found to permeate throughout the subject; extensively spread. "Pervasive disrespect for the president in the press belied his popularity in the polls."

foment

to bring about, incite, nurture, promote the growth of. "A certain unrest was fomented by the silent but obvious presence of the opposition party."

perfidious

disloyal, treacherous, especially in a relationship. *Perfidy* (treacherousness) is the noun. "…a politician who, perfidious equally in marriage and politics, was steadfast only in self-concern."

presumptuous

overstepping bounds, going beyond what is proper, taking undue liberties, forward in behavior. "The phrase, 'at the risk of being presumptuous,' usually precedes some totally inappropriate remark that takes the risk completely out of the presumption—it guarantees it.

swarthy

having a dark complexion. "…one side of the room bright with hopeful and shy farm girls, and the other dark with equally hopeful but far less shy farm boys, swarthy and coarse after a summer spent in their fathers' service among older farmhands."

bespoke

custom-made; made to order. "…a dapper man, wearing what was obviously a bespoke suit."

vouchsafe

to bestow, concede, or furnish, but in a condescending, begrudging, or stooping way: to deign.

The Vocabulary

pretentious
> making claims to an undeserved or unachieved status, or a too-obvious signaling of one's higher station. "Pretentiousness" is the noun, not "pretense." "To him, people who understood his art silently were morons, and those who understood it out loud were pretentious. Some of us thought is was a sham, however, and were merely accurate."

ineffable
> incapable of being verbally expressed. "An ineffable, morose fatalism had taken hold of Mann's two characters, and they nurtured it between themselves for decades until its prophesy was fulfilled."

pique
> vexation, especially from vanity or a perceived slight. "Generals, one might note, may yield to vanity and pique…and all the other foibles of proud men." [Eliot A. Cohen in the *Wall Street Journal*, April 19, 2006.]

ennui
> an unproductive, self-obsessed feeling of disillusionment, borne perhaps of boredom or sloth. "The fashion models practice hard at their off-camera ennui, their $1500 per hour perhaps grinding them down to it, or the drugs."

defalcation
> misuse of funds, or defection. Certainly not to be used in a context where it could be confused with "defecation," as in "Bromberg's defalcation left a stench that would stay with the firm for years."

raconteur

one who is very good at telling stories, especially anecdotes. "As a raconteur of the old (modesty) school, he told his stories in the first person and was always bested by his subjects."

ingratiating

calculated to curry favor or indebtedness, or having that effect. "The great thrust of elective politics seems to be ingratiating oneself to varied narrow interests at the expense of self definition."

sapient

wise and discerning. "…his failure to heed my sapient advice is the sole reproach to his otherwise superb book." [Christopher Hitchens, "The Grub Street Years," *The Guardian (UK)*.]

beg

As in "to beg the question"…to assume in one's discussion of an issue that the question has already been decided; begging the question is one of the many argumentative "fallacies," i.e. screw-ups in reasoning. Not to be confused with "inviting the question" or "raising the question," but very often confused anyway, especially in the popular press.

obtrusive

sticking out or protruding, obvious in a showy way. "In the famous photo, Sophia Loren's reluctant attention has been drawn to some more obtrusive parts of Jayne's features."

egregious

conspicuously bad and/or offensive, flagrant. "Thus, Lichtblau offers a lengthy series of instances in which individuals were made the victims of egregious violations of due process and basic rights." [Gabriel Schoenfeld, "In the Matter of George W. Bush *v.* the Constitution," *Commentary*.]

histrionic

relating to actors or the theater; "histrionics" is the noun, only seen in the plural, as in "spare me the histrionics!"

androgynous

having both male and female traits; once an insult when applied to either sex, but nowadays who knows. "The androgynous Boy George both died *and* faded away." See *hermaphroditic*.

cupidity

excessive desire for riches; lustfulness. "In satisfying his cupidity, he made himself master of all but his simplest desires."

implacable

impossible to placate or appease; unmovable in one's position or aggression; "implacability" is the noun. "'Will you stop, Dave?' So the supercomputer HAL pleads with the implacable astronaut Dave Bowman in a famous weirdly poignant scene…" [Nicholas Carr, "Is Google Making Us Stupid?," *The Atlantic*.]

colloquy

a formal conversation. "It wasn't the double-exposure effect of the last half-minute's talk that had dumbfounded him, for such incidents formed the staple material of Welch's colloquies." [Kingsley Amis, *Lucky Jim*.]

deprecate

to detract from, deplore, disapprove of. "When she started to deprecate little things in me that were no doubt congenital—the cock of my right eyebrow, for example—I suspected we were history, but only in hindsight did I know it: and thus it is with history makers."

lugubrious

sad and gloomy; mournful, dismal; applied commonly to such animals as bloodhounds and jilted lovers. "Lugubrious forest" is a poor usage, but often seen. "…eyes of a lugubrious cast, eager for more sad tales to stoke their smoldering gloom."

cynosure

the center of attraction or attention, that attracts admiration. Not to be confused with *sinecure*!

sinecure

a position or office that has no real power. "Nominally Anderson was V.P. of Change Management, but it was widely known in the company that this was just a sinecure."

virago

woman of great stature or strength, especially who is overbearing and scolding (see *termagant*).

rectitude
> rightness, correctness, especially moral. "Moral rectitude" is a trite and perhaps redundant usage.

perpend
> to reflect on or consider carefully; ponder.

derisive
> causing or meriting scorn (thus an act can be derisive, and it can also be described as derisive); mocking or jeering.

effusive
> gushing, with great outpouring of emotion; done with too-great a showing of emotion.

nominal
> in name only; very slight. "For a nominal fee…" is a common usage.

empirical
> derived from observation or experiment, as opposed to what is theorized or hypothesized. Verifiable by observation.

recalcitrant
> obstinately defiant of authority or restraint; resisting guidance.

violaceous
> of the color violet.

vernal
of the spring, or occurring then.

effluvia
offensive exhalation or smell; an invisible but apparent discharge of vapor. Often used to describe prose (see *afflatus*).

incertitude
an exhibition of uncertainty, absence of conviction ("...was likely to adopt a look of incertitude whenever confronted with a choice, however easy.")

pejorative
depreciatory, disparaging, deprecating. Also, tending to make worse. "I wanted to say that progress had 'stagnated' instead of 'stalled,' but I though that might sound pejorative."

abrogate
to annul, do away with, especially by authoritative action. "This action by the court abrogates the treaty." Not to be confused with *arrogate*.

propitious
being of good omen, presenting favorable circumstances. See *auspicious*.

spurious
bogus, inauthentic, false, forged, fake, counterfeit.

didactic
intended to teach. Often used pejoratively in describing a person who presumes to instruct others.

The Vocabulary

descry

to catch sight of, to suddenly see. Compare to *espy* (to see suddenly and in a hidden fashion from a distance). Confused too often with *decry*.

"A faint, veiled sign of continuities

That outward eyes can never quite descry."

(H.P. Lovecraft, "Fungi from Yuggoth.")

decry

to openly deplore or condemn. "Many attended her wedding reception—freely enjoying the free drinks—despite their earlier having decried her obvious pregnancy."

ostensible

open for view, displayed; alleged. "His ostensible good intentions" implies that he does have good intentions, and they are apparent. "His ostensibly good intentions" means the viewer has doubts.

ostensive

alleged or seeming; ostensible.

limn

to portray or draw; to delineate; to essentially portray or describe something. "Taken as a whole, this evidence limns the crime from start to finish."

espy

to see at a distance and recognize. "I could see to the next street and espied my man rounding the corner toward me."

dualism

theory that reality is composed of two irreducible elements or modes, e.g. good vs. evil, natural or nurtured. This is a philosophic term, much misused in common usage as in "the dualism of his intentions." Probably should have used "duality."

recrudescence

new outbreak of a feature or activity after a period of inactivity or abatement. Applied to symptoms of a disease, for example…or an eruption.

intercalate

to insert among or between existing elements or layers. "Two new commands were intercalated into each subroutine."

bight

a bend or curve in a geographic feature (such as a shoreline or mountain range); a bend or loop in a rope. "In the shimmering distance, trees and jacales stood along the slender bights of greenland pale and serried and half fugitive in the clear morning air." [Cormac McCarthy, *All the Pretty Horses.*]

ersatz

cheaply imitating the real thing: phony. "…the tawdry glitter of ersatz jewels on a pretender."

maudlin

slobberingly, overly sentimental. "…a maudlin drunk, pawing at my sleeve and telling me what a good, good friend I've been."

puerility

child-like behavior (not always a pejorative!). Adjective is *puerile*.

phantasm

product of fantasy. i.e., what one sees or imagines in the fantasy, as opposed to the fantasy itself. One has a fantasy, one sees a phantasm.

surreptitious

done or acquired by stealth or clandestine means. "…a surreptitious raid on the ice-cream compartment…"

tortuous

winding, twisted; not straightforward. "…A tortuous path through dense underbrush…" Yet another word whose meaning is being perverted by major-network news anchors who pompously use it when they should be using "torturous." Although both words have the same etymology, for the moment at least they have different meanings.

guile

deceitful and treacherous cunning (*guileless* is its opposite); manipulative intent. "A newborn has no guile; he cannot be spoiled by catering to his crying, for he cries out of a real need and is not trying merely to manipulate his parents: that comes later."

sanctimonious

affecting piety, righteousness, or an act thereof. "The President did his sanctimonious Bible-clutching only when the cameras were rolling; otherwise, it was held out of sight, and out of mind."

sardonic

bitter, scornful, mocking. "Sardonic laugh" is a trite usage.

conducive

tending to cause or bring about. Verb is *conduce*. Often used in the negative: "...not conducive to my comfort."

erudite

learned; obtained chiefly by learning.

bruit

to discuss a future event as being imminent or eventual; to widely rumor. Usually used with "about." "It is bruited about in Washington that the Iraq Study Group...will recommend turning to Iran and Syria to...bail out the U.S." [Eliot A. Cohen in the *Wall Street Journal*, Oct. 20, 2006.] Pronounced "brute."

insidious

awaiting to entrap, subtly harmful.

invidious

tending to injure the reputation or stature, or to cause envy. "I would stand next to Michelangelo's David, but I would be afraid of inviting invidious comparisons."

revile

to subject to verbal deprecation. "...reviled for his devotion to old-line Liberalism, in an age of mere Libertarianism."

The Vocabulary 109

opprobrium

something that brings disgrace; disgrace arising from some shameful act.

atavism

the re-appearance of a trait that has been gone for a while; a throwback. *Atavistic* is the adjective. "There may be an atavistic longing for quasi-divine kingship that surfaces in unsettled times." [Camille Paglia, "Real Inconvenient Truths," in *Salon.com*.]

indemnify

to protect against loss or injury; to make compensation for same. "I'm happy to climb this ladder to get your cat—but will you indemnify me against any injury, whether from the climb or from the cat?"

solipsism

theory or belief that the self can know nothing but its own modifications and that the self is the only existent thing. "...the solipsism of the young and arrogant, who find it impossible to imagine what is beyond their experience."

thrall

a servitude or obedience. "It has liberated the modern-day counterparts of *Mad Men's* secretaries and housewives from their thralldom to male sexuality, and it has freed men from their otiose masculinity and combativeness." [Sam Schulman, "The Television Show that Says You're Better Than Your Parents," *Commentary*.]

otiose

lazy; useless. "...it might be argued that [the principle]...was otiose, on the ground that the question it was designed to answer must already have been answered before the principle was applied." [Alfred Jules Ayer, *Language Truth and Logic*.]

plangent

having loud reverberating sound; having a plaintive or expressive quality. "Plangent ringing" is a hackneyed and perhaps redundant usage. "In a moment he said, without quite succeeding in keeping the plangency out of his voice, 'What am I supposed to do...'" [Kingsley Amis, *Lucky Jim*.]

contrite

acknowledging and sorry for one's transgression; grieving and penitent for one's sins or shortcomings. Not to be confused with "trite," but you wouldn't guess it from listening to certain evening-news anchorpersons.

abysmal

bottomless, hopeless or wretched. Like an abyss!

analeptic

having stimulating or restorative powers.

mendacity

a falsehood or lie; untruthfulness in behavior. *Mendacious* is the adjective. "At Turtle Bay, 'never again' has become a ghastly and mendacious cliche." [Jonathan Kay, "Organization Man," in *Commentary*.]

vacuity

an empty, inane thing; empty of ideas. *Vacuous* is the adjective.

sui generis

one-of-a-kind (alone in its genus!). "Or perhaps it will be admitted, however grudgingly and belatedly, that there is something sui generis about Islamist fanaticism: something that is looking for a confrontation with every non-Muslim society in the world and is determined to pursue it with the utmost violence and cruelty. [Christopher Hitchens, "Isolationism Isn't the Answer," in *Slate.com*.]

alarum

an alarm, but especially a signal warning of danger: a call to arms.

fulvous

of a dull, brownish yellow: tawny.

nimbus

radiance or cloud around a god or goddess when on earth (often used rather broadly); also a type of cloud formation. "The rest of the journey requires the articulation of a broader vision...a vision of conservatism, not only a nimbus of populism." [Yuval Levin, "The Meaning of Sarah Palin," *Commentary*.]

debar

to bar from having or doing something; prevent. Not to be confused with *disbar*. "He thought this profoundly true and, debarred from saying so, was at a loss what to reply." [Kingsley Amis, *Lucky Jim*.]

dolorous

caused, or marked by, expression of grief or sorrow.

brigand

one who lives by plunder; a bandit, especially one of a band of them.

canthus

either of angles made by the meeting of upper and lower eyelids.

amatory

of, relating to, or expressing sexual love.

fulsome

disgusting and offensive in its insincerity ("fulsome praise"). Not to be confused with wholesome, although some news readers have done so.

celerity

speed, quickness of action, esp. in completing work. See *alacrity* (promptness in work), *legerity* (quickness of mind). "It was a wonderful display of exactly-regulated celerity." [Patrick O'Brian, *The Yellow Admiral.*]

protean

variable, readily assuming different shapes or roles (like Proteus!). "For all of Nansen's protean accomplishments, it was the harrowing journey of the *Fram*...that gave his life story real drama." [Hampton Sides, "1000 Days in the Ice," *National Geographic.*]

divertissement
> a short performance within another performance (for example, the ballet sequences that used to be in Hollywood and Broadway musicals, R.I.P.).

dudgeon
> a state of sullen anger. "As soon as I spied her through the doorway I could see that she was in a fine, high dudgeon, obviously having already heard the news that I was bringing and ready to snap at the bearer."

stanch
> to stop or check in its course; also, a variant of *staunch*. "The boy tried to stanch the flow of tears as his playmates turned to see why he had fallen."

gouache
> type of painting using gum, or a technique thereof.

putsch
> a secretly plotted and sudden attempt at overthrowing a government.

legerity
> quickness in movement or action, especially quickness of thought.

educe
> to evoke or elicit; to bring out or draw out.

excrescence
> abnormal or immoderately large outgrowth or enlargement: a protuberance, like a wart.

diaspora
> a dispersion abroad (as in the Jewish Diaspora); the spreading of something homogeneous into its surroundings.

verst
> a Russian unit of length, about 2/3 of a mile.

apterous
> lacking wings, as in the dodo bird or the prehistoric apteryx. "In the comfort of her apterous schoolgirl days…"

impalpable
> incapable of being felt or touched; also, not readily discernible; obscure to the mind. "…something of which he was a mere symbol, something monstrous and impalpable, a timeless and faceless mass of immemorial horror…" [Vladimir Nabokov, "That in Aleppo Once…"]

lachrymal
> of or marked by tears. "…the lachrymal finish to his farewell address."

bombastic
> pompous, grandiloquent language that makes a show of itself.

censure
> strong disapproval and criticism, especially official; a rebuke.

The Vocabulary

iconographic
> a visual illustration; having an image that typifies a larger set. "...an iconographic eagle, crudely drawn on the back of the pilot's flight jacket..." Very close to *iconic,* which is more akin to a best example or prototype than to to a typical example.

portentous
> pompous; heavy with self-esteem. Not to be confused with *pretentious*.

scaraboid
> beetle-like.

hoary
> gray or white with age; venerable, ancient. "...the hoary old financial house of Scrooge and Marley..."

corvine
> crow-like. "Ichabod Crane, corvine and covetous..."

aspirate
> as a verb, to suck something out of; as a noun, that substance moved by aspiration.

coeval
> existing in the same period, having the same age or duration: a contemporary. "...having more maturity than his coevals..."

ictus
    recurring stress or bout in a rhythmic or metrical series of sounds. "The benched player's feet, otherwise motionless, twitched regularly with the ictus of the drumbeats…"

comminuted
    pulverized, reduced to small particles.

iridescent
    displaying a reflection of many colors, like an oil slick or rainbow.

immanent
    (philosophical term) taking place entirely in the mind, or within a specific domain of reality or discourse; inherent. *Immanence* is the noun. Not to be confused with *imminent* (about to occur). "Deists believe that the Supreme Being is immanent in natural objects."

polemic
    As a noun, an argument against a specific doctrine or belief; *polemical* is the adjective.

vertiginous
    causing vertigo; dizzy or giddy; inconstant; rotating. "He sat on the bed for a moment to recover from his vertiginous exertions…" [Kingsley Amis, *Lucky Jim*.]

condign
    fitting or appropriate; deserved, esp. regarding punishment. "…the inevitable and condign snub, after so many in the other direction."

vibrancy (also **vibracy**)

the quality of being vibrant, i.e. vigorous and vital and energetic. "This election was stolen for reasons of internal survival and long-term regional strategy by a regime confident enough to snub not just a U.S. government promoting impotence as moral virtue but [also] those allies in Europe who regularly jet in to offer cooing paeans to the vibracy of Iranian democracy." [Mark Steyn, "Iran and US," *steynonline.com*]

bibulous

inclined more to drink rather than not to drink alcohol. "...the bibulous Ted, never publicly hiccuping but always on the verge of it."

sibilant

sounding like an "s" or "sh." "A sibilant murmuring arose from the crowd."

quotidian

everyday, ordinary, commonplace. "Most tweets are viewable by all; they join a stream of tweets from around the globe—a ticker tape of quotidian detail." [Michael Agger, "What Are You Doing? The Allure of Twitter, the Latest Web Sensation," in *Slate.com*.] "For me, beer or wine with dinner and the chance to admire the beauty of women are among life's quotidian joys; I missed them." [Joshua Muravchik, "My Saudi Sojourn," *Commentary*.]

ratiocinate

to reason in an especially methodical way.

asperity

severity, as of a scene or person; harshness of manner, acrimony. "Early on, my great-uncle had accepted the uncontrollable asperity of his features, and had decided to vigorously counter this with the openness of his manner."

analecta (also **analects**)

a collection of passages excerpted from literature (these are both singular...)

enfetter

to bind in chains, as in a prison, esp. by the feet (with fetters).

asperse

to vilify, to make malicious charges (to cast aspersions...).

dissimulate

to disguise one's true feelings under a false appearance. See *dissemble*.

dissemble

to hide or conceal something under a false appearance; to make a false show of. Not to be confused with *disassemble*! "[The horse's] undistracted eye stayed fixed upon the dissembling foe, and the gravity of his horse-expression made the matter one of high comedy." [Owen Wister, *The Virginian*.]

rime

crust, or encrustation; icy crust formed by freezing rain on a surface.

chimerical

existing only as the product of wild fancy or unrestrained imagination; unreal; fanciful.

opalescent

reflecting a milky, iridescent light; appearing lit from within.

amphoric

like an amphora (ancient-Greek vase), having round body and a slender neck.

anapest (or **anapaest**)

in meter or verse: having two short beats, followed by one long one, or two unstressed followed by a stressed.

liturgy

rite or body of rites prescribed for public worship, especially Christian.

carmine

a rich scarlet, vivid red.

patronymic

name derived from the father, usually by affixing a suffix (e.g., Johnson, Nilson), or relating to same.

Proustian

literally, of or relating to Marcel Proust. But more commonly: of or relating to Proust's major theme, i.e. the decline of an aristocracy and its replacement with something more common and prosaic.

racemose
>in botany, a kind of branching pattern; having a structure composed of clusters of another structure.

commingle
>to cause to be mingled or blended. "To commingle funds" is a common usage. "...because no relation of a dream can convey the dream-sensation, that commingling of absurdity, surprise, and bewilderment..." [Joseph Conrad, *Heart of Darkness*.]

quatrain
>a unit or group of four lines of verse.

palpate
>to examine by touch ("palpation" is the noun, i.e. the act of palpating).

defenestration
>the throwing of a person or thing out a window. "It is a comforting fantasy of mine to eliminate all annoyances by defenestration, whether they be objects or people."

egalitarian
>of or promoting human equality, especially social (as opposed to athletic, financial, etc.).

maleficent
>working in, or producing, harm or evil; baleful.

inculcate
> to instruct or impress upon the mind of another by frequent and regular drill; to instill.

concupiscence
> ardent desire, especially sexual; lust.

inflorescence
> flowering; how a flower is arranged upon its stem.

concierge
> staff member attending at an entrance or at a desk, with assorted duties.

anent
> about, concerning. "...an inquiry, anent his non-payment."

nonce
> the present or singular occasion, pursuit, purpose, or use. Usu. seen as "for the nonce," e.g. for the moment, for the occasion.

supplicate
> to ask humbly or earnestly for something.

beseech
> to supplicate but with an urgency attached. "I beseech you!"

reprobate
> a shameless and morally lapsed person; one without moral scruples.

rousant
    tending to rouse; roused.

corposant
    St. Elmo's fire (i.e. the discharge of light at a prominent point of a ship or plane, or sometimes on power lines).

consonant
    being in agreement, accord, or harmony.

concomitant
    at the same time "...the concomitant arrival of my brother"; one who accompanies, esp. in a subordinate or incidental way.

recusant
    one who dissents; one who refuses to obey or accept authority (compare with "recalcitrant").

postulant
    a petitioner, especially one awaiting admission to candidacy or an order.

execration
    an act of cursing or denouncing; a loathing. *Execrable* is the adjective. "This of course brought vehement execrations upon my wretched head, and I made a hasty exit."

exposit
    to expound upon a subject, talk at length (performed by an "expositant"!)

litigious
> inclined to sue; disputatious or contentious.

enchase
> to set with gems. "The tools of migrant hunters...the dreams enchased upon the blades of them." [Cormac McCarthy, *Cities of the Plains*.]

palliate
> to reduce the seeming violence or excess of; to cover by excuses and apologies. "...an attempt to palliate their ongoing rush to conflict."

incult
> not cultivated; coarse, unpolished, or unrefined. "...an incult, but inspiring, choice to lead Poland."

inculpate
> to incriminate, accuse of guilt. The opposite of *exculpate*.

concrescence
> a growing together of parts; an increase by the addition of particles. "...the slow, inevitable concrescense of crud beneath the high chair."

concinnity (also, **concinuity**)
> harmony and fitness in design, or in literary style, especially in relating the parts to the whole. Adjective is *concinnate*. "...and the concinnate belt that pulled the outfit together."

tumefy
> to make swollen. See "tumescent" (swollen).

slattern
    an untidy, slovenly, grimy woman; prostitute or slut.

fictive
    imaginary, fictional, feigned; of, relating to, or capable of imaginative creation. "...Clinton's fictive parsing of the word 'is.'"

eponymous
    having the name for which another thing is named. As in "the eponymous David Copperfield," referring to the character, and the fact that the book is named after the character.

phalanx
    a tightly packed group of people; a body of troops in close arrays.

purl
    flowing gently to or around something; also, having a sheen like golden thread (not to be confused with "pearly"). "...the high water purling around the trunks of trees."

rill
    a very small brook or stream; to flow like one; to run on.

scabrous
    difficult, knotty (a scabrous problem); rough to the touch; covered with scabs; salacious.

purlieu

an outlying area or neighborhood; a place where one hangs about; a haunt. In the plural (i.e. *purlieus*): one's boundaries. "...the West End, the purlieu of his fall from virtue."

vagaries

eccentric, extravagant, or unpredictable actions or notions. Although the word is encountered most often in the plural, it certainly is used in the singular: "Through some architectural vagary, his bedroom could only be approached by way of a large bathroom..." [Kingsley Amis, *Lucky Jim*.]

clangor

a loud and jumbled noise; a loud racket. "Dixon guessed...that this must be the pacifist painting Bertrand whose arrival with his girl had been heralded, with typical clangor, by Welch every few minutes since tea-time." [Kingsley Amis, *Lucky Jim*.]

crenulated

having a top or edges that are puffy, like broccoli or cauliflower, especially minutely so. "...the crenulated ears of an old boxer." Not to be confused with *crenellated* (like the top of a castle wall).

gimlet

having a penetrating, driving, or piercing quality. "He looked at her with a gimlet eye, practiced and unwavering."

cortege

followers or attendants trailing behind an important person: a retinue or entourage. "Jackson's cortege has shrunk in parallel with his cache."

madeleine

a thing that evokes a memory or forgotten emotion. "For every big-city in the United States there is a name—the *Chicago Daily News*, the *Washington Star*...the *St. Louis Globe Democrat*—that serves as a Proustian madeleine, instantly conjuring up the memory of a beloved comic strip or an elegiac sports columnist or a hard-bitten crime reporter." [John Podhoretz, "The News Mausoleum," in *Commentary*.]

fastness

a stronghold; a hiding place. "...a grizzly hibernating in some sylvan fastness."

decollete (or décollete)

clothed so that the neck and shoulders (strictly speaking) are visible, but nowadays meaning also that the dorsal surfaces of one's breasts are exposed as well. (Noun is décolletage.) "And this lent to her appearance an air of being decollete, singularly at variance with her otherwise prudish ensemble." [Owen Wister, *The Virginian*.]

compendious

containing or briefly stating all the essentials of something larger; showing efficient use of time. "...getting rid of their wealth in the most compendious manner known to man..." [Patrick O'Brian, *Master and Commander*.]

indurated

having become firm or hardened, more firmly established. "...indurated factions grown ever more purblind by their smallness."

The Vocabulary

zeitgeist

the spirit or zen of the times, or that is characteristic of a generation or era.

declaim

to recite, as part of a formal program or as an exercise in elocution; to state loudly or to inveigh ("declaim against..."). *Declamation* is the noun.

recuse

to excuse oneself from participating in a decision, on the grounds of personal interest or non-partiality. "The judge had to recuse himself when his long-lost son came before his court."

schadenfreude

the pleasure one feels at the misfortunes of (certain) others. "Unavoidable, and utterly satisfying, a welcome feeling of schadenfreude bloomed warmly in my belly as she told me about the stalled career of my boss's former boss, a first-class prick."

brio

enthusiastic vigor and vivacity. "...a tenor of such brio as has not been seen in many years on this stage."

jerkwater

relating to a remote and insignificant town, usually rural. "...they were just a couple of hinds from some jerkwater town."

fractious

inclined or tending to make trouble: unruly. "I was in a fractious mood after a night of sleeplessness."

mawkish

excessively and objectionably or childishly sentimental: maudlin.

fey

doomed; foreboding calamity. Fairy-like. "The fey art director is gay, but no one can even imagine such a thing, and his friends keep trying to set him up with women." [Sam Schulman, "The Television Show that Says You're Better Than Your Parents," *Commentary*.]

necrotic

dead, especially a dead structure in a living thing. "...a healthy empire, but with necrotic institutions where unnourished by liberty."

cognoscenti

those who are in the know; those having, or claiming to have, specialized or superior knowledge or tastes. "We were cheered by the crowd but jeered by the cognoscenti." Singular is *cognoscente*.

bloviate

to blather on self-importantly, at length. Often used, and quite accurately, in describing the speech of politicians.

conflate
> to combine two concepts into one, or to confuse a property of one with another. "It is not too difficult nor too appropriate to conflate 'surrender' and 'appeasement.'"

synecdoche
> a broad category of figures of speech or idiom in which: something general represents something specific, or vice versa; a material represents the part made from it, or vice versa; a part represents the whole, or vice versa. (Examples: the use of "caffeine" to represent "coffee," as in "I need to grab some caffeine," when really coffee is the intended acquisition. Or, "Man, you've had too much coffee," when in fact it is caffeine that he has had too much of. Pronounced "sin-EK-do-kee.") "He jeered at the pair's rotten taste and aesthetic lapses, which he treated as synecdoches of their political transgressions." [Sam Tanenhaus, "Remembering Leslie Fiedler," in *Slate.com*.]

apperception
> introspective self-consciousness. Chiefly used in the field of psychology.

atrabilious
> inclined to melancholy by nature; peevish. Close to *bilious* (peevish and ill-humored).

embouchure
> the fitness of one's mouth muscles to play a particular wind musical instrument. Not to be confused with *embrasure*, but often done anyway.

embrasure
    an opening in a thick wall, for a window or door; a slot in a wall or parapet for firing weapons through.

elision
    the act or an instance of omitting or suppressing something; "elide" is the verb. "The elision of this event in Roberton's brief history of Clinton's presidency was further evidence of his political leaning."

bistre
    a grayish-yellow brown color. "To the south the thin green line of the river lay like a child's crayon mark against that mauve and bistre waste." [Cormac McCarthy, *Cities of the Plain*.]

rictus
    the mouth opening, or an opening resembling a mouth.
        "Atop the asphalt
        Still air feeds its chrome rictus—
        An Edsel rolling."

sejant
    sitting as a lion or dog (or a gargoyle) sits. "As she hauled her load of books up the library's entrance steps, dreading another afternoon of intellectual turmoil, the lions to either side seemed to mock her in their stony, sejant serenity."

propine

a gift, especially of money for drink. As a verb, to give as a token of friendship. One imagines a common character of W.C. Fields's seeking a propine among his many acquaintance at the bar.

persiflage

good-natured banter; idle talk, small talk; palaver. "...the air alive with the persiflage that comes from drink and good expectations."

asseverate

to assert or affirm with vigor and earnestness.

cumbrous

cumbersome. "...gave one of his cumbrous skips." [Patrick O'Brian.]

leonine

of or relating to a lion, resembling or characteristic of one.

aerie

a nest of birds or a dwelling that is on a high place.

topiary

relating to the decorative trimming of a tree or bush, especially to resemble an animal.

radix

the base or root of something.

bagatelle

a trifling, unimportant thing.

friable
   easily crumbled or pulverized; brittle. Not to be confused with *fryable*, thought by many to be an essential property of eggs and potatoes.

obverse
   as an adjective: facing the observer or opponent; having a base narrower than the top. As a noun: the reverse of something. "Ibuprofen is always a painkiller, but the obverse is not true."

physiognomy
   the art or practice of reading one's character and temperament by examining the contours of his face. Once thought to be a science!

annotation
   the making of explanatory or critical notes, as in the margin of a book or manuscript.

exegesis
   an orderly and/or critical explaining or proof of something, especially of a text. (One who is good at this is an *exegete*.) "...the exegesis of his thesis" is a common phrase used in humor by waggish professors of Freshman English.

saturnine
   melancholy and solemn; gloomy and ponderous. "Saturnine disposition" is a common usage.

The Vocabulary

succor

as a noun: relief, aid; that which furnishes relief in a time of stress. As a verb: to give relief or aid.

fatuous

silly or inane; especially smugly, foolishly, and unwittingly so. Noun is *fatuity*, sometimes also *fatuousness*.

nacreous

of or like mother-of-pearl (nacre). "...her nacreous complexion, with the blush of youth shining from beneath."

interregnum

strictly speaking: the time during which a throne is vacant; but generally, a lapse in a continuing function; hiatus.

galvanic

tending to shock; electrifying (like a galvanic cell battery....); tending to raise one's interest. "...the galvanic scene in the final act, where it seems that everybody got skewered, regardless of whether they were Hamlet's friends or foes."

galvanizing

tending to fortify or spur to action.

solicitous

showing concern; giving a high degree of care or attention; giving excessive and hovering care or attention in order to curry favor.

rapine

forcible seizure of property; pillage or plunder.

peevish

eannoyed, upset, or irritated by trivial things; querulous in temperament or mood; fretful; perversely obstinate.

scrupulous

upright, conscientious; attentive to the littlest details (*punctilious*). Note that *scruple* is a minuscule thing or part, an *iota*. "Having scruples" means ethical, with conscience, with consideration.

numinous

supernatural, mysterious; holy. Appealing to the higher emotions. "While others were preoccupied with work and family, he was preoccupied with the numinous…he would have made more money using his degree, but baking pizzas gave him time for his thoughts." See *noumenal* (unknowable by the senses).

contravene

to go or act counter to; to contradict. "…to contravene the regulations."

fuggy

stuffy or humid. "…the fuggy air in my grandmother's parlor."

connivent

converging but not fusing together, like sets of wings on an insect. "…connivent ribbons of highway." Not to be confused with *conniving*.

The Vocabulary 135

variegate

    to vary, give interest or color to. "…a display of green vegetables, variegated here and there with several types of red peppers."

neurasthenia

    nervous (i.e. mental?) condition in which one feels exhausted and/or listless. "By the 1890s Victorian America was intensely preoccupied with the sport as a new male proving ground and a remedy for the neurasthenia of the age." [Sally Jenkins, "The Team That Invented Football," *Sports Illustrated*.]

protreptic

    a speech or utterance designed to instruct or persuade. "…the dinner-table protreptics of my grandfather."

contretemps

    an inopportune, unforeseen occurrence, especially an embarrassing one. "He was met with a slight contretemps when his ex-wife entered the restaurant just as he was dangling a necklace in front of his latest pretty young thing."

ancillary

    auxiliary, subordinate.

arrogate

    to seize for oneself without right, especially a seizing of a privilege or power. "The young LBJ arrogated to himself the decision of which visitors his boss would see and would not see."

apotheym
> a pithy saying, an aphorism.

vaunt
> to boast of, brag of something. "You missed it—so much for your vaunted powers of observation!"

odalisque (also **odalisk**)
> a female slave, especially in a harem. "…in hopes that she would be made odalisque upon exposure to this new cologne of his."

parvenu
> one of the newly rich, an upstart not yet accepted by others in one's new class. "Claridge…recounts in fascinating detail the efforts of parvenus like the Vanderbilts to seize the mantle of civic leadership from established families like the Astors." [Jonathan Kay, "Post Modern," *Commentary*.]

fubsy
> chubby and squat. "…a suburban middle-middle-class rancher, complete with a blacktop driveway, a lawn gnome, and fubsy little bushes under each window."

gustatory (also **gustative**)
> relating to the sense of taste. "Gustatory delights" is hackneyed among headline writers in the Foods sections of the newspapers.

excurse
> to digress (make an excursion); a digression.

diadem

    a crown worn specifically as a sign of royal power or dignity. "…a titan of industry, surrounded by the assistants and functionaries that were both his diadem and his weakness."

surety

    the condition of certainty, assuredness; of being sure. Something that is beyond doubt (a surety).

warren

    a crowded tenement or district; a place where game animals (especially rabbits) are kept. "…the West Bank, a warren of mutually hostile factions united in their hatred of those who just want to move forward."

scrannel

    harsh and un-melodious; strident. "…the squawk of his scrannel voice leaping from my headset."

goodish

    almost good; as good as. "The fish was goodish caught, but still not landed."

torose

    knotted in appearance or form; also, cylindrical with ridges and bulges. "…his eyebrows, torose with thought."

torus

a smooth, rounded protuberance, especially from a load. "A pinkish-beige torus of belly overflowed the top of her jeans and flattened as she pressed against the counter."

amanuensis

a secretary, copyist, stenographer, clerk. "Watson: Holmes's assistant, foil, and sometime-amanuensis."

dotage

state of feeble-mindedness and/or decline in mental faculties, especially in old age. "In his dotage" is hackneyed. Note that *dotage* is far from being the same as *doting* on somebody (i.e. showing excessive fondness), but alas one hears this nowadays anyway.

regnant

ruling, reigning; dominant or widespread or prevalent. Often used after the noun it modifies, e.g. "the cat regnant." "They are the regnant topic of conversation all across the political establishment and have been for some time." [Christopher Hitchens, "Rushing for the Exit," in *Slate.com*.]

bailiwick

one's special domain of authority or expertise. Literally, where the bailiff presides. "His bailiwick, the arcane world of Grecian pottery."

paralogism

something fallacious, not following rules of logic. "His argument, a paralogism if ever there was…"

The Vocabulary

preternatural

beyond that of nature; extraordinary. "...Jane Austen's preternatural grasp of human motivation and response is what makes her stand out among even contemporary novelists of manners."

blowsy (or **blowzy**)

being coarse and ruddy of complexion; disheveled, frowzy, bloated.

revenant

one that returns from death or long absence. "Churchill, ever the revenant, once again raises his voice in the current debate over the merits of appeasement."

frisson

a moment of shudder or thrill felt upon some occurrence. "No one knows quite how Irish and gay politics got so comprehensively entwined, though personally I suspect it's something to do with the homoerotic frisson of *Lord Of The Dance*." [Mark Steyn, "Hillary on Parade," *SteynOnline*.]

pettish

fretful, ill-tempered, peevish; petty in one's reactions.

emulous

jealous, eager to pass another in station or success.

recumbent

lying down, especially in rest.

prolix

wordy to the point of tediousness. Noun is *prolixity*. "I think of [this book] as it should have been, with its prolixities docked, its dullnesses enlivened, its fads eliminated, its truths multiplied." [H.W. Fowler, "Dedication," *A Dictionary of Modern English Usage*.]

emendation

a correction of something as a way of improving it. "...emendations to the preface."

insular

literally, of an island: isolated, detached; of a narrow nature. "But then one of the reasons for his own later relapse into insularity was his unvanquishable fear of getting on an airplane." [Christopher Hitchens, "One Fraught Englishman," *The Atlantic*.]

ordure

excrement, manure; something filthy or repugnant.

evince

to show evidence of; to reveal or to manifest. "...the canyon's walls evincing eons of the patient wear of flowing water."

trope

a figure of speech; the use of words or expression in a figurative or metaphorical sense, or as hyperbole. "I already know something about "the speech" and its Lincolnian tropes." [Christopher Hitchens, "No Regrets," Slate.com.]

doyen
> the senior person of a body or group; the oldest one in a category or highest ranking. "...Ted Kennedy, doyen of the Eastern congressional contingent."

lustrum
> in Rome, the ceremonial purification of the population every five years following the census; a five-year period.

approbation
> an expression of commendations or warm praise. "...an event met with much approbation."

leaven
> as a noun, something which lightens or enlivens; as a verb, to cause to lighten or become enlivened; in baking, to add an agent that causes air bubbles, such as yeast or baking powder. "In those early days, conversations about the war were invariably leavened with naive anticipation that it would soon be over."

emprise
> an adventurous enterprise, especially in the cause of chivalry; boldness. "...must admire the emprise of his campaign, especially after he was expected to fold."

flagitous
> villainous, vicious, cruel; market by outrageous scandal or vice.

tope
    to drink intoxicating liquor to excess.

trichoid
    resembling a hair; covered in hair or bristles.

meliorism
    belief that the world will get better and that man can aid its betterment. A person believing this is a *meliorist*.

meliorate
    to make better. "...to melioriate the situation."

odeum
    a small theater or concert hall; not to be confused with *odium*.

odium
    state or fact of being subject to hatred or repugnance as a consequence of one's actions. Compare to *odious* (arousing odium).

mufti
    civilian clothes. "Obviously on his day off, the general appeared today in mufti."

scrobiculate
    having shallow grooves or pits. "...the peach seed, scrobiculate and dark."

festal
> of a feast or festival. "The peasants spent their precious free time making festal decorations."

fulgor
> *fulgence, refulgence*—a dazzling glowing or shining.

gimcrack
> cheap and showy; tawdry; having no real value. As a noun: something gimcrack! "'How are you,' he asked, keeping up the gimcrack friendliness." [Kingsley Amis, *Lucky Jim*.] "…Barack Obama's stimulus package -- a mammoth, chaotic grab bag of treasures, toys and gimcracks." [Camille Paglia, "A Rocky First Few Weeks," *Salon.com*.]

batrachian
> of or relating to a frog or toad. "Removing his reading glasses, the judge looked down at the offending prosecutor with a batrachian calmness."

sepulture
> the act of burial; a sepulcher (coffin). "A crowd was present sorrowfully at his sepulture, but happily not present at his disinterment."

rubicund
> tending to a healthy red or ruddy complexion. "He dropped onto his bed, exhausted after the effort—rotund, rubicund, and seeming (at the moment) moribund."

tenebrous (also **tenebrious**)
> forbidding, dark and gloomy. *Tenebrific* means causing gloom.

inanition

emptiness, lack of vigor; lethargy, exhaustion, depletion. *Inane* is the adjective.

abeyance

a state of suspension or having been put aside. "Few golf-haters fail to mention golf's tradition of festive pants, even though until recently such attire was in abeyance." [John Paul Newport, "Thanks, Golf Haters—Now Be Quiet," *Wall Street Journal*.]

crepuscular

of twilight; dim. "In this light, and in my mood, the library carrels seemed like crepuscular little havens for the unenlightened and benighted."

poesy

poem or body of poems; poetic inspiration.

spoliate

to despoil or plunder.

licentious

lacking moral restraints, especially sexual; disregarding rules.

mellifluous

smooth and sweet, flowing as honey. "She watched his teeth come ever nearer to her neck at the same time his mellifluous words soothed her agitation—and so she did nothing."

epicene

having characteristics of the other sex; effeminate; sexless.

accretion

process of growth or enlargement; concretion (solidification of particles into a whole). "Her hull showed an accretion of barnacles."

roborant

something that strengthens or restores. "I'll believe I'll have a little sip of whiskey—but just as a roborant, mind you." *Roborative* is the adjective.

obtest

to plead; beseech or supplicate.

tumid

swollen, enlarged, bulging, especially if a body part.

velleity

the lowest level of volition; the mere inclination. "The tangle of bills and sub-bills, the rhetoric of imperatives and velleities swirling about Congress, remind us of the evanescence of conservative doctrine." [William F. Buckley, in *National Review*.] "Even in this monastic seclusion...a fur coat stirred his carnal mind, and with the faintest velleity in the world he regretted that he had never known a girl in one." [Patrick O'Brian, *Richard Temple*.]

nonpareil

having no equal; without peer. "A woman of nonpareil sweetness and subtle backstabbing should go far in this organization."

penury
    extreme poverty or privation.

bacchante
    a female follower of Bacchus: a party girl. "He was caught *en flagrante* with a bacchante from one of those hanging cages at Club 21."

xenophobia
    fear and/or hatred of strangers or foreigners.

tergiversate
    to desert a cause, party, or faith.

lenity
    mildness, leniency. Not to be confused with *levity*.

despiciency
    a looking down upon; the act of viewing something as despicable; contempt. "It was bad enough that I couldn't forget that I had screwed up royally, but my parents' ever-mindful despiciency made living at home nearly unbearable."

puisne
    inferior in rank, often used ironically ("a puisne warrior"). Pronounced "puny."

hector
    to intimidate by blustering or personal pressure. "In popular myth, Emily Post is cast as a hectoring fuddy-duddy, holding forth on the proper

way to serve tea or address a foreign dignitary." [Jonathan Kay, "Post Modern," *Commentary*.]

rescision

the act of rescinding, i.e. taking back something previously offered; annulment or cancelation.

redress

(as a verb) to set to right, to mend. (as a noun) relief from distress; reparations. "...redress of grievances" is a common usage.

prorogue

to defer or postpone; to adjourn or terminate a legislative session. "Pelosi kicked C-SPAN out of the building and effectively prorogued the Republican attempt at keeping Congress in session in any publicized manner."

billet

a chunky piece of wood or bar of metal, especially used as starting material for something else; an official order for troops to be privately housed. "Every house had two or three British soldiers billeted there—most of them crude ingrates who demanded to be fed at great and unremunerated expense to the poor tenants."

encomiast

one who praises. *Encomium* is the praise itself. "The contemporary encomiast Bernal Diaz del Castillo wrote of the Spaniards' mad climb up Yopico, 'Oh! What a fight...it was a memorable thing to see us all streaming with blood and covered with wounds and others slain.'" [Victor Davis Hanson, *Carnage and Culture*.]

encomium

glowing praise. "...Scanlon, whose besotted encomium may constitute Brown's final caress in this vale of tears..." [Caitlin Flanagan, "Sex and the Married Man, *The Atlantic*.]

hegemony

preponderant influence or authority, especially of one nation over another.

palatinate

the territory of a palatine, i.e. a high officer of a palace or feudal estate.

weal

a sound, healthy, or prosperous state; the general well-being. "Bush's prescription drug plan, as well-intentioned as it might have been, proved to be just another cynical vote-grab that would further erode the weal and longevity of that mythical and ever-distant budget surplus prophesied by the enthusiastic bean-counters of his predecessor."

vassal

one in a subordinate position.

emolument

the profit arising from an office or employment, in the form of a perquisite or complimentary offering. "One might gather that this expectation of emoluments would attract optimists into the ranks of Licenses and Inspections agents, but it seemed rather to attract rank cynics."

rotary

a traffic circle. "New Jersey rotaries are nearly extinct, although one encounters them still on remote two-lane highways where traffic is light."

ancien regime

a system or mode no longer prevailing (more specifically, the political and social system in France prior to the French Revolution).

pensum

a chore or task assigned as a punishment, especially in school. "Writing 'I will not talk in class' 100 times on the chalkboard was preferable, as a pensum, to sharpening pencils, because it provided multiple opportunities to grandstand for the class when the teacher turned his back."

apercu

an immediate impression or insight, especially a discerning one; a brief sketch. "This sentence does a lot of work, especially in its second clause, while that coda about Europe (somewhat inelegantly tacked on, perhaps) shows that James revisited the apercu and thought about it in the light of Chile and South Africa." [Christopher Hitchens, "The Omnivore," *The Atlantic*.]

scrutator

an observer or examiner.

martinet
    a strict and/or rigid disciplinarian; one who demands adherence to rules. "...the dean of students, a martinet disguised in the disarming corduroys and tweeds of a beloved professor of classics."

quodlibet
    whimsical combination of familiar melodies or texts. Example: insertion of "Pop Goes the Weasel" into another musical work.

pottle
    a container holding two quarts; or the stuff contained in it. "...between us we drank a pottle of the stuff."

monody
    an ode sung by by one voice, in Greek tragedy; an elegy or dirge.

gloze
    to minimize or to gloss over; to underplay. "His glozing and seemingly offhand answer failed to deter us from what we viewed to be a deserving matter."

tutoyer
    to address familiarly.

manqué
    just short of, or frustrated in fulfillment of one's aspirations or talents. "...a poet manqué, now well versed in burger-flipping."

benighted
    overtaken by darkness; existing in a state of intellectual, social, or moral darkness. "...benighted deliberations, undertaken by cynics and destined to counter the aspirations of liberty."

malaise
    an indefinite feeling of debility or discomfort, often as a precursor to illness; a general depression.

incarnadine
    having the color of flesh; blood-red. "The fields of battle were littered with the incarnadine reminders—bits of clothing, broken blades, and stained dirt—of the dear price that was paid to both punish and indulge the vanities of ambitious men."

must
    musk; a needed item (exigency); a fruit juice that is being fermented.

lutanist
    a lute player.

undine
    a water nymph.

valetudinarian
    a person of weak or sickly constitution, especially one whose chief (and morbid) concern is his own invalidism.

genuflexion
: the act of kneeling.

lubricity
: wantonness or lewdness; slipperiness in character; shiftiness or instability. Adjective is *lubricious*.

lithophanic
: stone-like. "The judges' faces, relentless and dour, seemed to float above the bench like some lithophanic bas-relief of disapproval."

turpid
: marked by baseness or depravity; not to be confused with *torpid*. Noun is *turpitude*.

gloam
: twilight. Same as *gloaming*.

flavid
: yellow in color.

paladin
: a champion of a cause, especially in chivalry.

varisized
: of various sizes.

instauration
: the restoration after a decay or collapse; the establishment of something.

simulacrum

an other-worldly resemblance; a representation, imitation, or imaging of something real. "My father...was invited to a Hungarian simulacrum of 'The Drones,' the club where Wooster and his friends disported themselves." [Alexander Cockburn in an introduction to P.G. Wodehouse's *The Code of the Woosters*.]

disport

to carry on in a light and carefree manner, intent on amusing oneself.

inutile

not of any use (i.e., the opposite of *utile*).

rufous

reddish in color.

viatic

pertaining to travel or a path.

priapic

phallic, especially in excited state; ready for sex. "It's beloved by Emmy voters, suckers for the hambone acting of...William Shatner as the pompous, priapic Denny Crane." [Ken Tucker, "Boston Legal," *Entertainment Weekly*.]

raffish

of a flashy vulgarity or crudeness; rakish, marked by careless unconventionality. "...his raffish tipping of everybody in the place, from the parking attendant to the dishwasher."

leporine

of or relating to rabbits or hares. "...his leporine eagerness to take a handout."

crepitate

to make a crackling sound.

talus

rocky debris, or a slope formed from same. (Also: the anklebone.)

pensile

hanging or pendant; drooping.

tsigane

a gypsy.

circumflex

bending around something. "...sad, cracked columns with circumflex vines that spoke of decay and defeat."

argus

a watchful guardian; a hundred-eyed monster from Greek mythology.

The Vocabulary

explodent

explosive. "...his explodent anger, wide-ranging and untargeted."

remise

to give, grant, or release a claim to; to deed something.

purling

to eddy or swirl, as in waters; the sound made by such. "...purling waters of the little brook."

fatamorgana

a mirage.

logodaedaly

the building of elaborate or labyrinthine words. "*Antidisestablishmentarianism*, an exercise in logodaedaly." See *daedal* (a labyrinth).

gnosis

immediate, intuitive knowledge of a spiritual truth attainable through faith alone; practitioners would be *Gnostics*.

peristyle

colonnade surrounding a court, or the space enclosed by a collonade.

noumenal

something unknowable by the senses, but rather by the intellect alone.

bowdlerize

to skew the meaning of a work or text by removing portions, especially the racier portions. See *expurgate*.

expurgate

to remove vulgar or obscene portions of a work or text.

feuilleton

a popular novel; a short, familiar or broadly appealing literary work; secton of a newspaper devoted to short literary works.

precis

a concise summary of essential points or facts; abstract.

compendium

a listing of essential facts that functions as a summary—as opposed to an abstract.

puling

whining, whimpering. "Dear little souls: I remember them as poor puling little objects, fit only for bait." [Patrick O'Brian, *Blue at the Mizzen*.]

usufruct

the right to use or enjoy something, especially that owned by another. "Our rental property came with the usufruct of our neighbor's pool."

minikin

a small or dainty creature.

hustings

the proceedings of an election campaign; a place where political speeches are made. "The candidates' grit will become apparent in the hustings."

travails

hard labors—often used ironically or poetically. The verb is "travail," to labor hard.

brummagem

showy and cheap; like tinsel: meretricious.

Lucullan

lavish and luxurious.

fugal

of or relating to a fugue (musical form).

buncombe (also **bunkum**)

empty or insincere talk. Claptrap.

cuirass

armor that covers the chest and perhaps the back.

orotund

marked by fullness, strength, and clarity of sound. Also, bombastic or pompous in tone or presentation. Let context guide its meaning: "...a voice of such orotund splendor, a challenge to Caruso." Not to be confused with *rotund* (used primarily to mean "fat" ...but also sonorous).

gaminish

like a gamine—a girl who runs the streets; tomboyish. Also, having an elfin quality.

polymathic

possessing learning of an encyclopedic magnitude. Noun is *polymath*. "I once heard Susan Sontag, in conversation with Umberto Eco, define the polymath as one "who is interested in everything, and in nothing else." [Christopher Hitchens, "The Omnivore," *The Atlantic*.]

titubation

the stumbling gait of a crippled person or one with certain nervous conditions.

claudication

lameness, limping; a halt in the walking.

fuliginous

sooty, obscure, murky.

crotchet

a stubborn notion or stance (adjective is crotchety); a dodge, or devious device—particularly one that is unusual.

maunder

to wander slowly and idly; to speak indistinctly or in a disconnected manner. "...to avoid the tedium of...maundering afterwards." [Patrick O'Brian, *The Wine Dark Sea*.]

obloquy

abusively condemning language. Also, the condition of one whom is spoken ill of: ill repute.

subtile

subtle or elusive.

supererogatory

observed or performed to an extent not required; superfluous, nonessential. "...Jackson's blazer, with its supererogatory and alarmingly large school crest screaming from the breast pocket." *Supererogate* is the verb.

mortmain

the (perhaps oppressive) influence of the past regarded as controlling the present; also a legal term: a holding or property that can never be separated from the owning body. "He was just another trust-fund hippie, with the mortmain of grand-dad's trust fund ever-present like a cocked gun and an open wallet." "The mortmain of slavery, recent and unforgivable, forever darkens the bright plazas of Tripoli."

azoic

of or relating to a geologic time that predates life. "...the cold, azoic stare of the prosecutor."

oleaginous

resembling or having properties of oil; unctuous.

chilblain (or chilblains)
> soreness or swelling as a result of exposure to cold. "...came in from plowing the lower 40 with a bad case of the chilblains."

postprandial
> following a meal. "...a postprandial brandy would be most welcome, don't you think?"

midden
> a pile of manure; a refuse heap. "...archeologists combing through a village midden for artifacts."

sublunary
> literally, beneath the moon: terrestrial, of this world. "As I emerged from my fog, I felt a gun barrel nudge my neck with a sublunary coldness."

susurrous
> having a whispering sound. "...the night-time companion of my lonesome teens: the surging and susurrous wind as it played against the screen of my bedroom window."

congeries
> an aggregation or collection. Can be singular or plural.
> "...the books, in piles like twisted trees,
> Rotting from floor to roof—congeries
> Of crumbling elder lore at little cost."
> (H.P. Lovecraft, "Fungi from Yuggoth.")

The Vocabulary

stultify

to make useless or ineffectual; to cause to appear illogical, stupid, or ridiculous. "...the stultifying rebukes of our schoolmaster."

Sanhedrin

the supreme council and tribunal the ancient Jewish nation, in force at the time of Jesus of Nazareth.

homiletic

of or relating to a homily, i.e. a religious sermon. "These *de facto* editorials, couched in the vernacular of news reportage, were merely the homiletic and presumptuous rantings of a vain man."

interdict

to prohibit or debar, especially under authority; to place under a sanction. "Interdiction" is the noun.

egest

to excrete something or discharge from the body. "The sidewalks were dotted with the chalky remnants of chewing gum wantonly egested from the mouths of cretins."

baleful

deadly or pernicious in influence; foreboding evil; ominous. "Nobody wanted to get in the line of the Chief of Staff's baleful stare, for to get more than a couple seconds' worth was the kiss of death."

panoply
    a splendid and striking display; a protective covering; something worn ceremoniously. "His chest medals, ostesibly a panoply of virtue and virility, denoted nothing more than the extent of his graft in this most venal of banana republics."

philippic
    a discourse full of acrimonious invective; tirade.

argot
    the collection of idioms used by the underworld, especially privately; the language of a social group or class. "The person ... is the Rev. Susan Verbrugge of Blacksburg Presbyterian Church, addressing her congregation in an attempt—in the silly argot of the day—'to make sense of the senseless.'" [Christopher Hitchens, "Suck It Up," in *Slate.com*.]

tonsure
    the shaven crown of a monk; also, the rite of admission involving shaving one's head.

bawd
    one who keeps a house of prostitution (i.e., a bawdy house); a prostitute.

diapason
    a burst or outpouring of harmonious sound; the full range of a particular instrument or voice.

sobriquet

a fanciful name or epithet; a nickname. "…goes by the sobriquet of Gidget."

ukase

an edict or a dictate from an authority.

pother

fuss; a cloud of dusty smoke; mental turmoil. "All this mess had her in a proper pother."

cunctation

a delay. *Cunctative* is the adjective. "The line of questioning was just a cunctative tactic to allow the witness to prepare himself."

lagniappe

something given or obtained gratuitously as a good measure. "As he led her out the door, to dinner or a drink, Mum's boyfriend would flip a coin to me, as a lagniappe I suppose."

littoral

of the shore, especially the seashore. "…but if they wanted to be anything more than the Chile of North America—a long littoral ribbon caught between the mountains and the sea—they would have to prepare for a maritime struggle…" [Christopher Hitchens, "Jefferson Versus the Muslim Pirates," *The City Journal*.]

lenitive

something that alleviates pain.

nabob

a person of great wealth or prominence.

suzerain

an overlord; a dominant state controlling foreign affairs of a vassal state.

phiz

a face.

spindrift

sea spray. "...her features fogged by spindrift as she peered over the gunwale."

matutinal

of or relating to the morning. "...my matutinal shower."

peccant

guilty of a moral offense; violating a principle or rule. "We skirted unseeingly past the street of bawdy houses, hoping to avoid recognizing some morosely peccant face among the men gathered there.

pullulate

to germinate or sprout; to breed freely.

fugacious

lasting a short time (tending to flee...); evanescent.

estivate

to pass the summer in a state of torpor. Also spelled *aestivate*.

scrivener

a professional or public copyist (now extinct!) or writer.

oblations

religious offerings of inanimate objects. Not to be confused with *ablutions*, *ablation*, or *oblate*.

oblate

flattened or depressed at the poles—like the stone used in Olympic curling competition, or a pincushion.

wight

a living being or creature. "...a sound that would put fear into any wight large or small."

syncretism

the merging of different forms of belief or practice; the gradual adoption of one word to stand for several of its forms in common usage (i.e., "is" for both "is" and "are"). "...his recitation of soft-focus quotes from the Koran, Talmud and Bible came perilously close to a fuzzy New Age syncretism of "all religions are the same" -- which they unequivocally are not." [Camille Paglia, "Obama's Hit—and Big Miss," *Salon.com*.]

lucubration (or **lucubrations**)

laborious study, especially in the evening; (as *lucubrations*) studied or pretentious expression in speech or writing. "The housekeeper interrupted Holmes's lucubration to offer a cup of tea—he sent her away." "In those days my submissions were dismissed by reviewers as mere lucubrations, and rightly so."

puckish

impish, whimsical, mischievous.

alexandrine

a verse of twelve syllables, consisting of six iambic feet; of or relating to Alexandria, Egypt.

sough

to make a sighing, murmuring sound. "I held my head close to the window, to see the moon, and heard the night breeze soughing in the screen."

mistral

a violent, cold, dry northerly wind in the south of France.

compline

seventh and last of the canonical hours (in Catholicism).

risible

laughable; capable of laughing; disposed to laugh. "Posner may have accomplished a few things—such as helping to knock down the actuarially risible belief that there had been a hundred or so 'mysterious deaths' among people who supposedly knew too much..." [Thomas Mallon, "A Knoll of One's Own," *The Atlantic*.]

fascicle
> a bundle; one part of a book that is published in parts.

gobbet
> a piece of portion of something, usually of meat; a tiny morsel. "There I was, a ten-year-old with an adult jones, forever biking past her house in the vain hope of some gobbet of attention."

autarchic
> of or relating to self-sufficiency and or independence, especially of a nation or state; absolute rule. Noun is *autarchy* or *autarky*. "...her autarchic haughtiness."

maieutic
> of or relating to the Socratic method, especially in revealing latent meaning through questioning.

prescind
> to detach or separate (in the abstract) for the purpose of thought. "It became necessary in my thoughts to prescind the teacher from his classroom, and there he loomed suddenly ridiculous and pedantic."

etiolate
> to cause to appear pale, especially via lack of sunlight (as in a plant); to enfeeble, to make sickly, to take away the natural vigor. *Etiolated* is the adjective. "We would sometimes catch glimpses of her through the bay window, sitting in etiolated repose deeper within the room, waiting for something that never would come."

draconian
    extremely harsh or cruel: severe. "Draconian rules" is a common usage. (Also *draconic* sometimes seen as a synonym, but better used to mean "dragon-like.")

arrant
    thorough-going, confirmed; notoriously or outstandingly bad; unmitigated. "...an arrant brigand."

demarch
    a course of action, maneuver, usually diplomatic.

truckle
    to act in a servile manner: bend obsequiously. "...truckling servants who behaved as necessary to maintain their employment in the house of such a tyrant."

factotum
    an employee with various duties. "a family reduced to keeping one or two factotums, after having employed a much larger staff before the war."

sciolism
    a superficial show of learning; pedantry; lucubration.

soupcon
    a little bit; a trace. (Probably best not used orally, but pronounced "soup's own.")

suppositious

fraudulently substituted: spurious. When said of a child: illegitimate.

febrile

of or relating to fever; feverish.

descant

a contrapuntal melody. (As a verb: to write counterpoint.)

brinkmanship

the practice of pushing a dangerous situation to the limit—i.e., to the brink—before stopping.

natter

to talk much but say little. Vice President Spiro Agnew referred to some of his detractors as "nattering nabobs of negativism." [Attributed to William Safire, one of President Nixon's speechwriters.]

satrapy

the rule or dominion of a satrap, i.e. one who is actually serving another. "During the cold war, Poland was a satrap of the Soviet Union."

ursine

of or relating to, or resembling, bears. "...one got used to his ursine gait."

dengue

a certain acute tropical infectious disease, borne by mosquitos.

foofaraw

    silly fuss, or frilly finery. "...this is all knicknacks, doodads, and foofaraw."

scatological

    of or relating to the body's excretory functions, especially defecation; relating to excrement. "Snickering, scatological humor is common among schoolboys."

Procrustean

    marked by a disregard for individual differences (a la Procrustes…). "It's typical of today's Procrustean liberalism that it wants to destroy the depth and solidity of traditional consensus while demanding rigid superficial consensus on its own pet topics." [Joseph Sobran, "The New Taboos," UPI, sobran.com.]

callipygian

    having a beautiful rump.

steatopygian

    having a large rump.

apothegm

    an aphorism.

misericord

    relaxation of monastic rules. Also: a knife used to kill oneself, or another, when mortally wounded already.

The Vocabulary

sparge

to spray, especially into another fluid.

noetic

of or relating to or based upon the achieving or apprehending of an understanding through purely intellectual means, as opposed to empirical. "As a young boy he struggled to understand the meaning of his father's long absences, and his noetic concept of some 'other mother' in some other house was not far from the mark."

camorra

group united for dishonorable or dishonest ends; a cabal.

nodose

having many protruberances (nodes), or conspicuous ones. Pronounced with a hard "s" to avoid confusion with the renowned pick-me-up.

gasconade

boastfulness, bravado.

orison

a prayer. "...he would preemptively drop to his knees and bury his face in perfervid orison." [Christopher Buckley, *Losing Mum and Pup*.]

reliquary

container for religious relics.

lubricious

marked by wantonness: lecherous, salacious. Slippery…

palimpsest

a writing material that is or has been used and reused. "The billboards had been whited out…and through the paint could be seen a pale palimpsest of advertisements for goods which no longer existed." [Cormac McCarthy, *The Road*.]

conatus

a natural tendency or inclination. "…a conatus toward gambling, and gambling on anything."

reluct

to show opposition to: revolt.

glaucous

of a bluish-gray or bluish-white color; having a powdery, waxy coating that rubs off. "…far-off rainclouds, glaucous and menacing."

sapphic

(in poetry) relating to certain four-line rhythmic scheme. Also: of or relating to lesbianism.

alembic

a distillation device, but more often: a device that purifies or concentrates. "But of course inquiries into parents' concern for their children's education are quickly arrested by citing individual inclinations to come

The Vocabulary 173

up with alembics for their own philosophical system." [William F. Buckley, Jr., "Thanksgiving at the Buckleys'," *National Review*.]

pharmacopoea

a book or list of medicinal drugs; a collection or stock of drugs.

debouchment

the outlet of something. "...formerly a lush delta, the debouchment of the Mississippi in modern times takes the form of tens of miles of levee-bounded channel poking its way deep into the alluvial Gulf."

argent

the metal silver; also, a whiteness.

contretemps

an inopportune, embarrassing occurrence. "I had a little contretemps at the office today."

solecism

a blunder in speech; an ungrammatical construction; a faux pas. (Not to be confused with "solipsism.") "If we could say *our common friend* [instead of *our mutual friend*] our troubles would be over, but in England a real grammatical solecism is preferable any day to a fancied social solecism, and the risk of seeming to mean that the friend is vulgar or lower class is too embarrassing to be faced." [Kingsley Amis, *The King's English*.]

gulosity

greediness; gluttony.

janissary
    member of a group of fiercely loyal or subservient troops.

eristic (also, **eristical**)
    inclined to argue whether called for or not, and especially to use specious argument. "I am lapidary but not eristic when I use big words." [Headline of essay by William F. Buckley, *New York Times*.]

lapidary
    marked by very precise attention to detail, as when cutting stone or gemstones; of or relating to cutting stone or gemstones.

dauphin
    eldest son of the King of France.

viands
    articles of food: vittles.

advert
    to require attention to; to pay heed to. "A blister adverts to an underlying problem with the shoe."

harridan
    a woman with a reputation for being scolding and vicious; a nag.

pleonasm
    use of more words than necessary to denote mere sense: redundancy.

ebriety

the opposite of sobriety: drunkenness.

fulminate

to utter or send out with denunciation.

apprize

to appreciate or to value. Not to be confused with *apprise* (to tell).

outré

bizarre; unconventional; eccentric. "Is an outré paint job, like an unkempt lawn or a car on blocks, a blight on the landscape and a violation of middle-class norms?" [Virginia Postrel, "Paint of View," *The Atlantic*.]

fustian

pretentious writing or speech; a coarse, thick cloth. Not to be confused with *Faustian* (of or pertaining to a tale where one sells his soul).

emir

a native ruler in parts of the Middle East.

jocund

marked by or suggestive of mirth; jolly of disposition.

jocose

tending to joke, merry.

jocular

tending to joke.

icterus

jaundice.

suborn

to induce secretly to do an unlawful thing. "Suborn to perjury" is a common usage of this.

draconic

dragon-like. Not to be confused with *draconian* (harsh or severe).

empyrean

(noun) the highest heaven; ultimate heavenly paradise. Adjective is *empyreal,* not to be confused with *imperial.*

cuneiform

having the shape of a wedge; also, a typeface or writing hand composed of wedges.

scudding

to run before—or as if before—a gale; "...in Dad's yacht, scudding up to Newport."

ormolu

a brass made to imitate gold.

maenad

an unnaturally excited or distraught woman; a female participant in orgiastic rites. "At first Bill thought of Monica as just another plaything from the intern ranks, a willing maenad in the ritual routing out of the best and the un-wisest."

plica

a ridge or fold of skin.

banausic

merely mechanical and automatic in delivery or style: banal, dull, prosaic, staidly practical. "...one more banausic zombie of an English teacher."

trull

a slattern or trollop; a loose and vulgar woman; strumpet: prostitute.

frigorific

causing coldness or chilling. "She shot me a frigorific stare that brought an instant end to my anecdote."

glabella

the—one hopes—smooth prominence between the eyebrows, nowadays the nemesis of so many botox users.

mythopeic (or mythopoeic)

of or relating to the making of myths; preoccupied with myth; relating to myth. "...the mythopeic sum of his CEO career was at odds with the shabbiness of his domestic life."

hierophant
    one who explains or interprets mysterious things; an advocate or spokesperson. "Dan Rather never quite became the hierophantic pooh-bah that Cronkite was."

theriomorphic
    having animal form, or supposed so.

anthroposophy
    beliefs or belief system derived from theosophy (which claims one can know God or the soul as as result of a mystic's insights.)

surd
    (as an adjective) lacking sense or reason; irrational; voiceless; …"a surd piece by a deadened playwright." (As a noun) an irrational number; "I fear that I am excluded not only from the joy of prime numbers and surds but from the mathematics as a whole." [Patrick O'Brian, *The Hundred Days*.]

enfeoff
    to invest with a fiefdom; noun is *enfeoffment*. "In 20th-century Philadelphia, to become a building inspector was to become enfeoffed with the power to tax at will."

gadarene
    headlong, with strict consequences. "…her gadarene plunge into matrimony."

elytra

protective wings (as on a beetle).

gules

heraldic red.

ecchymotic

bruised (a result of ecchymosis, i.e. internal bleeding into subcutaneous tissue).

embonpoint

one's plumpness (stated in a respectfully oblique way). "His reputation precedes him even more so than his embonpoint."

leitmotif

a musical theme or melody associated (in a work, such as a movie or opera) with a specific character; a recurring theme.

straiten

to narrow; to put into a condition of hardship or distress. "...will finally take the full measure of the threat to its long-term survival and husband its straitened resources to address the threat..." [Jonathan S. Tobin, "The Madoff Scandal and the Future of American Jewry," *Commentary*.]

exordium

the introduction or beginning part of something, especially a speech or essay.

apodictic

relating to or expressing a necessary or demonstrable truth (in the philosophical sense) or an absolute certainty. A guy who asks for a "last cigarette" before the firing squad has chosen an apodictic adjective. See *ineluctable*.

demivierge

a female who readily engages in loose talk or "half sex," but does not give up her virginity. Probably can be applied to males also, but the gender of the word is feminine in original use. Used derisively more than in praise. "Bill Clinton, the demivierge of pot smokers…"

sciolist

one who makes a superficial show of his knowledge; a pedant. Pronounced "sigh-o-list." The noun is "sciolism." Probably pedantic in most uses.

Paraclete

the Holy Spirit.

spavined

lame (specifically, on a horse's hoof, having a bony enlargement due to strain).

gibbous

marked by convexity: protuberant. Also: used to describe the phases of the moon where the moon is more than half full. "…a gibbous moon seemed to follow us as much as to light our way."

suspiration

    a long, deep breath: a sigh.

ovine

    of or relating to sheep. Not to be confused with *bovine* (of or relating to cows)!

lacuna

    blank space or gap; cavity, pit or discontinuity in an anatomical structure.

gelid

    extremely cold: icy. "Her gelid stare induced me to seek another dance partner."

suppliant

    one who supplicates (who asks, humbly, for something).

calcined

    heated, as a powdery solid, while being stirred, to force some chemical reaction. "His was a hatred initially refined from tales of some ancestral injustice, calcined with the imagined slights of a paranoid adolescence."

parterre

    an ornamental garden, with paths for walking.

intrigant

    one who intrigues. "Camille, my intrigant of the moment."

droxy
a woman of loose morals.

mensuration
the act of measuring. Not to be confused with *menstruation*!

meninx
any of the three membranes that enclose the spinal cord and the brain.

doss
to bed down in any convenient place; a makeshift bed.

dyadic
coming in pairs, seen in pairs, twofold. "They're not partners...nonetheless, there is something dyadic about these two." [James Parker, "Brit Wit," *The Atlantic*.]

elysium
Greco-Roman heaven (the Elysian Fields); a place or condition of ideal happiness: paradise.

perfervid
extremely or extravagantly eager or fervent; impassioned or zealous. "...his perfervid attentions, like the searches of a puppy..."

cognate
related by blood; having a common ancestor; kindred. Related in origin (like some words). "Those heavens in whose forms men see commensu-

rate destinies cognate to their own…" [Cormac McCarthy, *Cities of the Plain*.]

propaedeutic

introductory or preparatory instruction. "My nephew professed an interest in coins, so I gave him an old penny collection as a propaedeutic."

misology

hatred or distrust of logic, reason, or enlightenment. "She was hard to argue with in any logical sense of the word—she reacted to both syllogism and analogy with a peremptory misology that brought one's train of thought to a sputtering halt."

pandect

comprehensive digest or complete treatise; as a plural: a body of laws or legal code.

decretal

an authoritative decree, especially from the Pope.

archaism

an archaic or old-fashioned word or expression in speech or writing, or in an art.

intestine (as an adjective)

internal or civic. "…intestine affairs of the state."

caesura

a pause in a line of speech or oration; a pause in some process. "Dixon stirred elaborately at his post, then twisted himself about looking for anything that might have had a share in causing this caesura in his journey." [Kingsley Amis, *Lucky Jim*.]

repine

to be discontented or low in spirits; depressed, dejected. To yearn after something lost and unrecoverable. "...old men sitting with their pints, repining for the powers and the challenges of their youth."

palladium

a safeguard. "...a weak judge, palladium of the tort bar." Also, one of the metallic elements!

primogeniture

in law, the right of the eldest child; the condition of being the eldest child of a pair of parents. "In my family, the seat closest to the stove, in winter, and closest to the door, in summer, was Hugh's by right of primogeniture as well as might."

amerce

to punish by an arbitrary fine, at the court's discretion. The fine would be an *amercement*.

nugatory

of little or no importance; having no force; invalid. "And why is such a nugatory issue a legal matter in the first place?" [Christopher Hitchens, "Free Scooter Libby," in *Slate.com*.] "Nobody outside a madhouse, he

The Vocabulary 185

tried to imply, could take seriously a single phrase of this conjectural, nugatory, deluded, tedious rubbish." [Kingsley Amis, *Lucky Jim*.]

plenary

complete in all respects: "...plenary authority." Full, or fully attended by all members: "...plenary session." "But the symbol of Saddam on the gallows is a symbol of justice pursued, even if plenary satisfaction is not possible." [William F. Buckley, National Review Online, Dec. 29, 2006.]

nostrum

a medicine unproven and secret; a quack remedy; a known but perhaps ineffective remedy for problems or evils.

litterateur

one devoted to the study of literature, or literary pursuits. Note two *T*s, not one!

stertorous

having a heavy snoring or gasping sound. "In my office I was continually distracted by the stertorous thrum of a closed-off ventilator."

ambit

an external boundary; a limit or scope, especially to influence or action. "...but also a powerful sense of safety to be found in the ambit of the family, which itself is bound by the wisdom and goodness of Babar and Celeste and their love for each other." [Meghan Cox Gurdon, "The Story of Babar and Kin," *Wall Street Journal*.]

adjure

to command or enjoin, especially solemnly; to appeal to or entreat.

entreat

to make an earnest request of.

ichor

the blood of the gods, i.e. what runs in their veins.

ballista

a medieval heavy engine of war; a catapult.

luculent

very easily understood or perceived: pellucid.

viscid

thick and adhesive, especially if a fluid: viscous. "...viscid attentions that transitioned quickly from solicitous to ingratiating."

uxorious

showing excessively submissive or devoted fondness to one's wive, or manifesting as much. "...self-assured to the point of abrasiveness, a non-drinker, and, once he had married Goldwyn Girl Gloria Delson, in 1945, steadfastly uxorious." [James Kaplan (writing of Sammy Cahn), "The King of Ring-a-Ding-Ding," *Movies Rock* supplement to *GQ*.]

habitude

a habitual tendency or behavior. "...and he spooned in his nightly boiled cabbage with habitude, if not relish."

demotic

in the manner of the common people; of the common people. "...they reluctantly saw that Kristol had found a memorably demotic way of encapsulating the sad fashion in which utopianism can collide with brute facts about the human animal." [Christopher Hitchens, "Farewell to the Godfather," *Slate.com*.]

darksome

dark, gloomy, somber. "...a low, squalid, shingled house, huddled half in and half out of the darksome forest beside it."

fabliau

a tale, especially medieval, containing ribald themes and generally concerning the lower classes. "...and at the bar, worn-out men exchanging the worn-out fabliaux of their youthful days."

neoteric

fresh; recent in origin, modern. "She appeared one day in our crowd—introduced to us by somebody I have forgotten—and as neoteric and exotic as she seemed, she was suddenly the center and the pulse of our group."

tendresse

fondness.

uranist

a homosexual.

pastiche
    something that combines varying and different elements—a hodgepodge. "…his dirty shirtfront a pastiche of the previous week's meals."

coruscate
    to sparkle; to emit flashes of light. "…the coruscation of diamonds in their glass cases."

favonian
    mild, lacking in any threat. Literally: of or relating to a west wind.

phocine
    of or relating to seals. "…her phocine repose…and figure."

dithyramb
    a statement or writing in an wildly enthusiastic manner.

glozening
    glistening. Not to be confused with *glozing* (tending to gloss over…).

scansion
    the analysis of verse in order to show its patterns, especially of meter.

decalogue
    a basic set of rules carrying the weight of authority: ten commandments, literally.

supernumary (or ***supernumerary***)

in excess of the proper or sufficient number; superfluous. "...a deep-seated insecurity that manifested itself aggressively, especially after the supernumary glass of wine." [Christopher Buckley, *Losing Mum and Pup*.]

etiology

the causes of an abnormal condition (i.e. of a disease); the study of causation.

adamantine

hardened, unyielding. "Her fluent mendacity, combined with adamantine confidence, made her truly indomitable." [Christopher Buckley, *Losing Mum and Pup*.]

deliquescent

melting away; dissolving; becoming soft or liquid gradually.

basilisk

a legendary reptile or dragon whose glance and breath are fatal.

syndicalism

the running of industries by workers, or advocacy of that, especially via strikes, slowdowns, etc. "Paris's subways over the years have descended to a sort of syndicalism where every management decision is subjected to a silent referendum, whose outcome is known only by the subsequent behavior of the workers."

chrysalis

the pupal stage of a butterfly or moth, when enclosed in a case.

rachitic

rickety; suggesting the condition of one with the disease rickets.

congener

a person or thing resembling another in nature or action. "CNN, and its congeners in the print media, all strangely seem at times to be acting on some universal impulse to make a specific point on the same day, independent of any specific news event."

purdah

a seclusion from other social classes; literally, the enforced separation of men and women as in some religions. "...the supercilious purdah of the elitists."

nates

the buttocks. "Jenkins took some birdshot in the nates and then promptly took a swig of brandy, never complaining of either; could be that it hit his hip flask."

dolor

sorrow or grief; mental anguish. *Dolorous* is the adjective.

ululation

howls or lamentations; wailing. "...heard her call amid the ululations."

seraglio

a large harem, or a sultan's palace. "...the drones, a seraglio of males, who neither collect the honey nor form the hive, but exist only for lazy enjoyment." [Thomas Paine, *Rights of Man*, speaking of Europe's arisocracy.]

incondite

crude or badly put together. "His last sculpture—er, construction—was an incondite sham, and as one would expect the critics raved."

preprandial

before a meal, or suitable for the time before a meal. "...his preprandial ablutions." After the meal would be *postprandial*!

venery

indulgence or pursuit of sexual activity, especially wantonly; hunting, or the game that is hunted.

eructation

the act (or art!) of belching. "Preprandial lip-smacking, postprandial eructations."

oculate

having features that resemble or are suggestive of eyes. Example: the spots on some butterfly wings.

neuralgic

having a pain along a nerve. "...complaining, habitually, about some neuralgic curse or another."

auscultation

the act of listening in order to diagnose: listening for body sounds as a diagnostic tool. "Commonly, when Mother and Dad were having one of their 'discussions' supposedly out of reach of our ears, my siblings and I would gather round a heater vent and listen in studied and experienced auscultation."

acidulous

slightly sour in taste or manner. "...my proposal was met with an acidulous frown from the boss."

pravity

wickedness, foulness.

inwit

conscience or understanding. "...the painter's strokes, animated by an inwit of his subject's pain."

moil

to slave away, to toil; to engage in drudgery. "...the moiling deckhands, polishing what had already been polished."

ludic

of or relating to play or playfulness. "...his continual and supposedly ludic comments about her ambitions began to grate."

agon

conflict between protagonist and antagonist, or between characters in general, especially in a work of literature.

The Vocabulary 193

anfractuous

full of windings and turns: tortuous. Compare to *fractious*.

sere

withered and dry. "She surveyed the horizon, her expression sere and troubled."

cerement

a death shroud: cerecloth.

obeisance

a gesture meant to express deference, obedience, or homage to another (example: curtsy or bow).

espial

the act of observing; a noticing or discovery of something visible. Verb is *espy*.

inamorata

a woman one is in love with, or with whom one is having relations.

porcine

pig-like. "In his middle-age affluence he had developed a porcine wabble."

doppelganger

one's double, or "twin," especially one that is other-worldly or ghost-like. (Often used derisively, as in "your doppelganger, Attila.")

pneuma
the soul, or vital spirit: breath of life.

rotograveur
a part or section of the newspaper in which pictures of the public or society are displayed.

tocsin
an alarm, especially one sounded on a bell. "In ringing the tocsin, moreover, leading Democrats spoke at least as assertively as leading Republicans." [Arthur Herman, "Why Iraq Was Inevitable," *Commentary*.]

conturbation
a disturbance.

conurbation
an urban region including surrounding towns and suburbs: a metropolitan area.

hind (as a noun)
a farm worker or obviously rural inhabitant; a country bumpkin.

veridical
truthful, veracious: genuine; in accord with reality. "Emerging from his timeless unconsciousness, he stretched his fingers across the dark space toward the cell walls in a search for some veridical hardness that might anchor him to the present."

canicular

of or relating to dog days (hot, humid days of summer). "The assembled screeches of cicadas overhead, a distant dog barking, screen doors slamming, a bus wheezing away from the corner—these formed the canicular background music to the unending summer mornings of our too-short boyhoods."

morganatic

a marriage between partners of unequal rank or wealth—especially where there is no possibility of wealth transfer to either the lower spouse or to descendants.

eudaemon (or **eudemon**)

a benevolent ghost or spirit.

charnel

a place where bones or the dead are kept (also: charnel house).

auspicate

to initiate or enter upon, perhaps in a ceremony, in a manner intended to ensure good luck.

antinomian

an adherent of antinomianism (the belief that faith guarantees salvation, regardless of one's adherence to moral or social law).

prevenient

coming before; anticipatory; antecedent. "It was always our custom, when home from school for the holidays, never to drink a brandy with Father without the prevenient glass of tawny port."

objurgatory

characterized by harsh scolding, rebuking. "He remembered his father, who until the war had always worn stiff white collars, being reproved by the objurgatory jeweler as excessively 'dignant' in demeanour." [Kingsley Amis, *Lucky Jim*.]

armature

a framework that supports a piece of sculpture; a protective covering. "Graham Greene…found Hitchcock's early films to be dramatically shallow, mainly because they lacked the dramatic armature of plot-based psychological development that Greene thought essential to storytelling." [Terry Teachout, "The Trouble with Alfred Hitchcock," *Commentary*.]

anile

of or like an old, doddering woman: senile.

murrain

a pestilence or plague affecting domestic fauna and/or flora.

murid

of or relating to rats or mice. Best not used when easily confused by the listener with "myriad," to wit: "There were murid little animals underfoot."

haute

fashionably elegant; high-class. "Haute cuisine" is a hackneyed usage.

Pelagianism

The teachings of Pelagius, i.e. the doctrine that man is free from original sin, and can be righteous through his own actions. Compare to *antimonianism*.

bedizened

excessively ornamented; showy or gaudy.

confect

to make by combining different materials or parts; to make a confection: concoct.

andante

moderately slow (a musical direction...).

irenic

conducive to, or operating toward, peace or reconciliation or (at least) moderation.

jingoism

extreme nationalism, especially resulting in a belligerent foreign policy.

conventicle

an assembly or meeting, especially unlawful in character or purpose. Example: a meeting of an outlawed religion or political group.

lumpen

separated, dispossessed, dissociated, or departed from one's class or intellectual roots; not conforming to its name. "There is a reason why the French Communist Party, which used to dominate the working class, the unions, and much of the lumpen intelligentsia, is now a spent force that represents perhaps 3 percent of the electorate." [Christopher Hitchens, "The French Reaction," in *Slate.com*.]

sempiternal

eternal (literally, always eternal!). "...and always the tide, coming ever anew but sempiternal."

emunctory

serving to carry waste from the body: excretory.

solon

a wise and skillful lawgiver or lawmaker.

enfilade

a group of objects appearing in single file and presumably vulnerable to strafing gunfire. "...little naked mesquite posts wandering singlefile away into the night like an enfilade of bent and twisted pensioners." [Cormac McCarthy, *The Crossing*.]

provenience

source or origin. Not to be confused with *provenance*. "A wealthy and hard-working grandfather was the provenience of both his fortune and his sloth."

recrement

waste material; worthless stuff.

dishabille (or **deshabille**)

a state of partial undress, or extreme casualness of dress; lounge-wear. "The whores, in their shabby deshabille, looked up from the shabby sofas where they sat." [Cormac McCarthy, *Cities of the Plain*.]

vectress

feminine form of "vector," in the personal sense, i.e. that person which bears something to a destination or direction. "...and she would prove to be the vectress of the most poignant of my disappointments."

fissiparous

tending to break away into parts.

relict

something surviving when all around has changed, especially a living thing: a widow for example, or a surviving species among a broader extinct group.

velutinous

velvety, or covered with fine soft hairs.

abulia (also aboulia)

impairment or abnormal loss of ability to make decision.

demulcent
> serving to sooth or soften. "Do nothing but drink demulcent barley water." [Patrick O'Brian, *Master and Commander*.] See *anodyne*.

costive
> slow and sluggish; constipated. "...of the grossest self-induced costiveness it has ever been my privilege to see." [Patrick O'Brian, *Master and Commander*.]

sortilege
> sorcery or witchcraft; the casting of spells. "Perhaps that was the secret of her sortilege." [Joseph Conrad, *The Shadow Line*.]

purblind
> lacking in vision or insight; sluggish in mentality: obtuse. "...a purblind refusal to look at the matter again, despite there being new evidence."

vaticinate
> to prophesy or foretell. Noun is *vaticination*.

clyster
> a thorough flushing, i.e. an enema. Used figuratively, as in "Man, what a clyster I got in my last performance appraisal."

mammothrept
> a spoiled child. "'And having seen the parents I am impatient to see this youth, the fruit of their strangely unattractive loins: will he be a wretched mammothrept?" [Patrick O'Brian, *Master and Commander*.]

crapulous (also crapulent)

marked by excessive drinking or eating; sick from excessive eating or drinking; drunk; tending to engage in excessive drink. "There was something about Miss Cutler's cornflakes, her pallid fried eggs or bright red bacon, her explosive toast, her diuretic coffee which, much better than bearable at nine o'clock, his usual breakfast-time, seemed at eight-fifteen to summon from all the recesses of his frame every lingering vestige of crapulent headache..." [Kingsley Amis, *Lucky Jim*.]

boltered

having a look of nearly-unrestrained wildness (as would a horse who is a bolter, i.e. one that tends to bolt or run away.). "...the boltered, staring look had gone." [Patrick O'Brian, *Master and Commander*.]

pied

patchy in color; splotched (piebald). "[It could be] all the colors of the rainbow, or even pied, for all [he] cared at this moment." [Patrick O'Brian, *Master and Commander*.]

flack

as a noun: a press agent or publicist. As a verb: to flap or flutter. "The red flag and pendant flacked overhead..." [Patrick O'Brian, *Master and Commander*.]

sectary

a sectarian; a dissenter from the church. "As a man of some learning, he is awkward company for our sectaries." [Patrick O'Brian, *The Wine Dark Sea*.]

syncope

a short lapse of consciousness. "Was the driver slumped in his seat, the victim of syncope, or had he suddenly got an idea for a poem?" [Kingsley Amis, *Lucky Jim.*]

impost

something that is imposed, like a tax, levy, or duty. Also, the weight one carries in a handicap race. "...and he is now one of those who...will receive the hated impost." [Patrick O'Brian, *The Wine Dark Sea.*]

daedal

ingenious or complex in design; intricate; as a noun: something that is so. "...a daedal of passages." [Patrick O'Brian, *The Wine Dark Sea.*]

hieratic

priestly, or relating to sacred functions. "...while the boy held up the reel with a hieratic solemnity." [Patrick O'Brien, *The Mauritius Command.*]

froward

oppositional and perverse, obstinate, perhaps by habit. "...an oppressed commodore, growing froward under ill-usage." [Patrick O'Brien, *The Mauritius Command.*]

postern

a small gate at the back or side of a structure. As an adjective: situated at the side or the rear.

shieling

a shepherd's hut. "I don't care if it's a mansion or a shieling— at this point I'll take it."

supererogate

to do more than is warranted, ordered, or expected. "…might have seemed a work of supererogation." [Patrick O'Brian, *The Wine Dark Sea*.]

idoneous

fit, appropriate, suitable, proper. "…no one could be more idoneous, fitting, or suitable." [Patrick O'Brian, *The Truelove*.]

thaumaturge

a magician; performer of miracles. "We are now quite clear of…your thaumaturge's territory." [Patrick O'Brian, *The Truelove*.]

scelerate

notoriously wicked. "…the scelerate Bonaparte." [Patrick O'Brian, *The Truelove*.]

titivate

to spruce up; make tidier or prettier. "…the captains of the guns and their crews titivated their pieces." [Patrick O'Brian, *The Truelove*.]

demesne

the land belonging to a manor or a country house.

myrmidon

    a follower who carries out orders without question. "...another one of his dependable myrmidons will doubtless be spinning it to the press this weekend."

irrefragable

    impossible to contradict or refute; indisputable. "Edwards is a good trial lawyer—he can produce an irrefragable argument on any issue, in support of either side."

empiric

    one who is guided by experience, as opposed to theory or teachings; a dishonest practitioner: charlatan.

aprication

    the practice of basking in the sun. "He attributed his notable longevity, and his deep wrinkles and skin-cancer scars, to his long habit of aprication."

minatory (also, **minacious**)

    menacing or threatening. "A moving vehicle was now, in his hands, a potential weapon of mass destruction far more minatory than anything in the arsenal of Saddam Hussein or Kim Jong-il." [Christopher Buckley, *Losing Mum and Pup*.]

piractical (also, **piratical**)

    of or relating to pirates. "...it had a piractical directness." [Patrick O'Brian, *Treason's Harbor*.]

mumchance
    silent due to stupidity or ignorance. "…these gentlemen were…a mumchance, melancholy class." [Patrick O'Brian, *Treason's Harbor*.]

missish
    appropriate to or characteristic of a young girl; prim or affected. "…no missishness, no bridling, no simpering." [Patrick O'Brian, *Treason's Harbor*.]

antiphon
    a short song or chant sung as a response during a religious service. "His pagan stomach…had gone on grumbling until the end of the first antiphon." [Patrick O'Brian, *Treason's Harbor*.]

coriaceous
    leather-like. "But he is a difficult, coriaceous sort." [Patrick O'Brian, *Treason's Harbor*.]

swinge
    to punish with blows; to thrash or beat. "In spite of the…swingeing fees, this provided him with a comfortable sum of money." [Patrick O'Brian, *Treason's Harbor*.]

frowsty
    having a stale odor; musty. "Never had he seen such a squalid crew—crapulous, down-at-heel, frowsty." [Patrick O'Brian, *Treason's Harbor*.]

scend
    to heave upward on a wave or a swell; the rising of a ship on a swell. "The answer obviously varied with the force of the wind and scend of the seas." [Patrick O'Brian, *Treason's Harbor*.]

rantipole
    characterized by a wild and unruly manner. "This rantipole hero..." [Washington Irving, *The Legend of Sleepy Hollow*.]

consist
    to be consistent, compatible, or in accord. (The common usage, of course: to be composed, to be made up whole from parts, e.g. "consists of.") "...that consist with one another in all their details." [Patrick O'Brian, *The Fortune of War*.]

nepenth (or **nepenthe**)
    a drug that eases grief, or induces forgetfulness of sorrow. "...the nepenth that had tided him over." [Patrick O'Brian, *The Fortune of War*.]

lickerish (or **lickerous**)
    eager to taste or enjoy; greedy, desirous. Tempting to the appetite. "A lively eye, and somewhat lickerous." [Patrick O'Brian, *The Fortune of War*.]

altumal
    of or relating to the sea, especially sea-borne trade; in the mercantile style, or the dialect of the mercantile class—especially that of low traders. "...the altumal simplicity of our diet." [Patrick O'Brian, *The Fortune of War*.]

dégagé

free and relaxed in manner or bearing. "Nothing could induce them to form in an orderly group, and they stood in dégagé attitudes..." [Patrick O'Brian, *Desolation Island*.]

prodrom (or **prodrome**)

precursor or precondition, or preliminary symptom. Plural is *prodromi* or *prodromes*. Chiefly a medical term. "The prodromi are such that I should be clear in my mind, if it were not for this period of latency." [Patrick O'Brian, *Desolation Island*.]

pule

to whimper or whine. "Were you to give way to melancholy, you would certainly pule into a decline." [Patrick O'Brian, *Desolation Island*.]

latibule

a hiding place or a lurking place. "One always imagines Tolkien's Gollum peering up from the murky gloom of some rocky latibule."

fetor

an offensive odor; stench. Not to be confused with *fetter* or *fetters*.

esculent

edible; suitable to eat.

limicoline [or **limicole**]

of or relating to shore birds. "He was intimately acquainted with what might be called the limicole world." [Patrick O'Brian, *The Letter of Marque*.]

capabarre

    the practice of using government property for private use. "...knows just about where to draw the line between culpable capabarre and traditional friendly accomodation." [Patrick O'Brian, *The Letter of Marque*.]

mansuetude

    gentleness of manner; mildness. "You will see Padeen's face return to its usual benevolent mansuetude..." [Patrick O'Brian, *The Letter of Marque*.]

impostume

    an abscess, or pustulent wound. "...hoping to deal with a possible impostume by that time." [Patrick O'Brian, *The Letter of Marque*.]

peripety (or **peripeteia**)

    a sudden reversal of fortune or circumstance, especially in a story.

farouche

    fierce, wild; seemingly subdued but with an air of deadliness. "Bow drawn, he eyed the target with a farouche confidence."

feculent

    having a foul content; fecal. "...the feculent curse of intellectuality." [J.D. Salinger, "Hapworth 16, 1924."]

barbican

    a tower or fortification near the entrance to a town.

castellan

the keeper or master of a castle. *Chatelain* is equivalent.

catholicon

a universal remedy; a cure-all; a panacea. "These [coca] leaves were his present...catholicon." [Patrick O'Brian, *The Nutmeg of Consolation*.]

seneschal

one who is in charge of servants. "...demoted quite gradually from chief of staff to a mere seneschal who marshals the secretaries without controlling any longer the President's inner circle."

consanguine

having identical or similar lineage; having a common ancestor. "The ganadero leaned back and studied them one and then the other. As if he'd been called upon to judge their consanguinity." [Cormac McCarthy, *The Crossing*.]

divagation

a wandering; a divergence or rambling. "My girlfriend's father poured himself a little glass of Madeira, and interrupted his lecture for a welcome divagation on the differences between port and sherry."

cerise

a deep reddish-purple; cherry color.

seigneur

a man of rank. "The prisoner wearing the fitted vest stood out as a seigneur amongst the usual run of hooligans in the Sunday-morning holding cell."

houri

a beautiful, seductive woman. "...she was a houri at the court of Thanatos, and had learned her darkness..." [Adam Hall, *The Quiller Memorandum*.]

thanatos

instinctive or innate self-destructiveness. Capitalized: a psychiatric term for self-destructiveness. "In the unequal battle between life and death...Eros has its part in warding off Thanatos..." [Christopher Hitchens, "Sons and Lovers, *The Atlantic*.]

gormless

lacking intelligence or vitality. "...re-nominating a dull-witted, gormless Boston aristocrat would be malpractice on the order of picking an accountant as your heart surgeon." [Jonah Goldberg, syndicated column, Jan. 18, 2007.]

threnody

a speech or song for something that has died; a dirge. "Thus 'A Whiter Shade of Pale,' which originally embodied sixties excess, becomes a threnody for a generation." [Mike Butler, in *Lives of the Great Songs* (Tim De Lisle, ed.)]

chiliast

one who believes that an ideal society or order (i.e., the Millenium…) is foretold and is coming, perhaps through revolution. "…the mullocratic chiliast who looks forward cheerfully to the end of the world of the infidels." [William F. Buckley, "Iran in Our Future," April 7, 2006, describing Iran's Ahmadinejad.]

clerisy

the educated classes. "In other words [the popular press says,] the intelligence community should be a sort of clerisy accountable to no one." [*Wall Street Journal* editorial, April 26, 2006.]

fillip

a goad or incentive. "…the official-secrecy faction within the state machinery has received a gigantic fillip from the press witch hunt…" [Christopher Hitchens, writing in *Slate.com*, April 24, 2006.]

viridity

inexperience arising from youth. "It is easy to forgive youths their viridity, but not their youth."

syncretic

fusing two different schools of thought, philosophy, religion, etc. "Whether this syncretic, tolerant, and expansive form of religiosity has a fighting chance in today's Egypt is an open question, but Mr. El Gendy is convinced it better represents the country's history than the strict and humorless version represented by the Muslim Brotherhood." [Bret Stephens in the *Wall Street Journal*, June 6, 2006.]

lineament
> feature or contour, an outline. "A history so intricately filiated will soon disclose lineaments of tragedy..." [Christopher Hitchens in *Slate.com*, Oct. 26.]

filiate
> (legal) to legally judge the paternity of a child; (popularly) to trace the connections of cause and effect between two things.

ruction
> a riot or uproar. "The ructions on the periphery of the Saudi lobby...obscure the extent to which...." [Christopher Hitchens, in *Slate.com*, December 18, 2006.]

obmutescence
> a state of muteness or self-imposed speechlessness. "Jud was a monologist by nature, whom Destiny...had set in a profession wherein he was bereaved... of an audience; therefore, I was manna in the desert of Jud's obmutescence." [O. Henry, "The Pimienta Pancakes."]

subfusc
> dark, drab, and somber, especially in color. "The Black Watch...'black' because of the subfusc colors of its Campbell tartan..." [Philip Howard in the Wall Street Journal, Dec. 26, 2006.]

hejira (also, **hegira**)
> a fleeing; a flight to escape danger and to seek more pleasurable surroundings.. "Oddly, with her aimless hejira over, she has attained per-

manent star status in the pictorial dynasty of doomed blond sex symbols." [Camille Paglia, "Camille's Back!" in *Salon.com*.]

glyptic

of or relating to the cutting or engraving of stone or jewels. "This kind of glyptic clarity stands or falls on...the draughtsmanship of the powerful forms and outlines..." [Howard Hibbard, *Michelangelo* (speaking of Michelangelo's *Doni Madonna*).]

tranche

a portion or division existing within a larger whole. "Add to this the rather peculiar fact that a huge tranche of voters—most recently as large as 40 percent—simply refuse to tell the opinion polls (who last time got everything calamitously wrong) how they intend to cast their ballots." [Christopher Hitchens, "The French Reaction," in *Slate.com*.]

panoptic

taking in everything in view; presenting a comprehensive view. "James...tries to show how tough and shapely were the commonsense formulations of Raymond Aron, for example, when set against the seductive, panoptic bloviations of Jean-Paul Sartre." [Christopher Hitchens, "The Omnivore," *The Atlantic*.]

inquorate

insufficient in number: not enough to make a quorum. "They then appealed to the Constitutional Court, which held that without them, the numbers would be inquorate..." [Melik Kaylan, "Trouble in Turkey," *The Wall Street Journal*.]

eleemosynary

intended as an act of charity; of or relating to; constituting charity. Chiefly a legal term.

invigilate

to keep watch. "A belief in a supreme, eternal, invigilating creator who knows what you think and do and cares about you…" [Christopher Hitchens, quoted in *The New York Times*.]

ventricose

swollen or extended on one side. "The Principal, a small ventricose man with a polished, rosy bald head, gave one of his laughs." [Kingsley Amis, *Lucky Jim*.]

locus classicus

a phrase from a classic or pivotal work of literature that is cited to illustrate a particular point one is making. "At least for people of my age, the Watergate disclosure is the ur-text, the compass point, the locus classicus of the press's earning the privilege it is granted by the First Amendment." [Christopher Hitchens, in *The New York Times*, reviewing Bob Woodward's *The Secret Man*.]

cozen

to deceive; especially, to acheive or obtain something by deceit. "…he had fallen into the painful weakness of trying to find proof that a real liking had at one time existed, even if it had existed alongside the interested cozening—something to show that he had not been deceived in quite every respect." [Patrick O'Brian, *Richard Temple*.]

The Vocabulary

glabrous

lacking protuberances or projections: smooth. "...he could see that the guard's pale, glabrous face was shining with tears." [Patrick O'Brian, *Richard Temple.*]

constuprate

to fornicate; to engage in a sexual act. "...at a certain level he wished they were not quite so perfect—that Barbara would betray a certain frumpishness, or Ludwig would be found constuprating the refugee servant." [Patrick O'Brian, *Richard Temple.*] No doubt closely related to the Yiddish "stup." Not to be used, of course, where its sound might reasonably be confused with "constipate," as in: "Somehow after I have spent lots of money on laxatives that don't work, I feel somewhat constuprated."

involution

the process of becoming more and more involved, twisted, intricate, complicated. "But simplicity vanishes with poverty: everything becomes involved, everything is a tortuous scheme. Nobody is less simple than a man long tried by want, as if involution were his last defence." [Patrick O'Brian, *Richard Temple.*]

djinn

a genie, i.e. a spirit taking human form. "He polished the underside of the messtray with the sleeve of his shift and ...he studied...the face that peered dimly out of the warped steel like some maimed and raging djinn enconjured there." [Cormac McCarthy, *All the Pretty Horses*]

increate

existing, but not having been created, i.e. always having existed. "He looked into those blue eyes like a man seeking some vision of the increate future of the universe." [Cormac McCarthy, *All the Pretty Horses*]

ataraxia [or **ataraxy**]

a state of calmness; peace of mind. "It is ironic that we scramble and fight all of our lives to achieve an ataraxy that can be attained also by simply not caring about it."

subvention

a grant of either help or funds. "Galloway's front organization, a "charity" known as the Mariam Appeal that campaigned against the sanctions on Iraq, had in fact received direct Iraqi subventions from the proceeds of the U.N.-sponsored "Oil for Food" program." [Christopher Hitchens, "The Galloway Papers," in *Slate.com*.]

comminatory

an official or formal reprimand or rebuke.

cataleptic

as a medical term: having no volition—i.e., cannot move limbs or move head, and limbs stay where they are put. In more common usage: totally lacking in initiative, unmotivated.

riant

producing mirth or gaiety. "...the room was decorated with a riant irony (said the interior decorator of his own work)."

The Vocabulary 217

clamant

tending to proclaim or announce itself (or oneself); loud and clamorous. "The clatter on the asphalt was tremendously effective: knives, forks, can-openers, pie pans, pot lids, biscuit-cutters, ladles, eggbeaters fell, beautifully together, in a lingering, clamant crash." [James Thurber, "The Car We Had to Push."]

plashy

having many small pools, as in a marsh or bottomland. "They had reached the plashy bottom, and a snipe got up with its usual cry…" [Patrick O'Brian, *The Yellow Admiral.*]

wrack

(as a noun) the remains of ruined or destroyed things; (as a verb) to cause ruin or destruction. "Wracked with guilt" is a hackneyed usage. "…familiar and congenial though this was—a kind of inverted homecoming, with the smell of sea and tide-wrack in their nostrils…" [Patrick O'Brian, *The Yellow Admiral.*]

fleer

(as a verb) to run away or swiftly vanish, especially away from danger or peril; (as a noun) a taunting or derisive look. "I have it in contemplation to grow a beard and put an end to these ill-timed fleers for good and all." [Patrick O'Brian, *The Yellow Admiral.*]

lycanthropy

the delusion that one has assumed the behaviors of a wolf or some other wild animal; the mystical power to assume the shape of a wild animal. "Please forgive me: it was only a weak, foolish burst of superstition...lycanthropy might be a better word, perhaps." [Patrick O'Brian, *The Yellow Admiral*..]

abattoir

a slaughterhouse; like a slaughterhouse. "I wonder how many people...have any idea what it means when compared with the insane proceedings of the totalitarian abattoir state that was Iraq until 2003." [Christopher Hitchens, "Something to Give Thanks For," in *Slate.com*.]

telluric

of the earth; grounded, solid, touchable. "...a text of telluric insight, free of the numinous ramblings that weigh down more common music criticism."

grimoire

a text containing imprecations, spells, magic, etc. "...leading one to speculate just what dusty grimoire he had consulted along his fortuitous rise to the top of the corporation."

memorious

capable of great and far-reaching memory.

teleological

of or relating to the belief that there is a purpose or directed end in natural processes. "But it's not just weathermen who use teleological explanations, ascribing purposeful behavior to inanimate objects." [Walter Williams, "Silly Talk," *Townhall.com*.]

acropper

characterized by failure or falling apart. Sometimes seen as "came a cropper." "Alas, Norman's good idea came acropper because he didn't control the rights to any of the top players in the world..." [A.G. Pollard, Jr., "The Big Golf Bust," *Hemispheres*.]

caracole

to move in a winding fashion. "A piece of wire sprang from some hole and hung caracoling about my ankle." [Owen Wister, *The Virginian*.]

alkahest (or alcahest)

the universal solvent purported by alchemists to exist, and sought by them. "A world construed out of blood and blood's alcahest, and blood in its core..." [Cormac McCarthy, *The Crossing*.]

slat

(as a verb) to throw or project forcefully; to strike. "...by the final afternoon of our journey, with Sunk Creek actually in sight and the great grasshoppers slatting their dry song over the sage-brush..." [Owen Wister, *The Virginian*.]

maculate

spotted, dirty, splotched. Opposite of *immaculate*!

dejections

secretions or results of bowel movements: turds. "...innumerable forms of vermin had gnawed or attempted to gnaw the superfine broadcloth or ruin the gold lace with their squalid dejections." [Patrick O'Brian, *21*.]

frigor
    coldness of the body. "...the gaze almost instantly followed by a feeling of unavoidable and certain death, cold death, followed by furious uncontrollable heaves and shameless vomiting, morbid frigor and despair." [Patrick O'Brian, *21*.]

hale
    (as a verb) to pull on: haul. "...stalking about the nightmare deck in their uncouth garments, uttering their brutish cries, haling upon ropes great and small..." [Patrick O'Brian, *21*.]

frippery
    showy, pretentiously elegant. "...a knowledge both acquired and to some degree...instinctive of the sea's very nature itself bears down all frippery land-based experience, however old." [Patrick O'Brian, *21*.]

benison
    a blessing or benediction. "[For Van Gogh] the hydrotherapy baths at the asylum...must have been a benison." [Oliver Bath, "A Week in Provence," *Forbes Life*.]

pukka (or **pucka**)
    representative of the best of its kind; of the best. "He engaged the firm of Butterfield and Robinson, the pukka bespoke travel service..." [Oliver Bath, "A Week in Provence," *Forbes Life*.]

Horla
    a supernatural being with human form, capable of controlling one's thoughts and action (by all accounts, taken from the short story, *Le Hor-*

la, by Guy de Maupassant). "Had he done all this himself [burned a hole in the bedclothes...]...or was he the victim of some Horla fond of tobacco?" [Kingsley Amis, *Lucky Jim*.]

guy

to mock and riducule. "And if any one thing undid Governor Palin...it was the merciless guying of her manner and personality by Tina Fey." [Christopher Hitchens, "Cheap Laughs," *The Atlantic*.]

embassage

one's standing as an ambassador or emissary. "Brand and Gervais, fellow countrymen, come to these shores in the embassage of two very different types of Englishness." [James Parker, "Brit Wit, *The Atlantic*.]

proscenium

the portion of a theater stage between the curtain and the orchestra pit. "...among the sudden slats of light that stood staccato out of the parted board walls, moving through those serried and electric prosceniums where they flared white and fugitive across the barn..." [Cormac McCarthy, *Cities of the Plain*.]

discalced

not wearing shoes; shod in sandals, perhaps for religious reasons. "They were discalced to a man like pilgrims of some common order for all their shoes were long since stolen." [Cormac McCarthy, *The Road*.]

siwash

rough and primitive in manner or setting. "...he rose and walked out and cut a perimeter about their siwash camp looking for a sign..." [Cormac McCarthy, *The Road*.]

patteran (also **patrin**)

markings or objects left by gypsies along a path to mark the way for followers. "...cairns of rock by the roadside. They were signs in gypsy language, lost patterans." [Cormac McCarthy, *The Road*.]

dolmen

a tomb formed by two upright stones and a capstone spanning them. "At a crossroads a ground set with dolmen stones where the spoken bones of oracles lay moldering." [Cormac McCarthy, *The Road*.]

molder

to decay into dust.

secern

to find distinction between two things; to discern differences. "...synonyms secerned, obsolete forms obelized, dubious usages dehorted, and catachreses condemned." [J. Arthur Greenwood, in an affectionate nod to H.W. Fowler (see the entry for *prolix*), in *Find it in Fowler's*.]

obelize

to mark a passage in a text with an obelus (an obelisk-shaped thing) to indicate a passage one considers spurious, doubtful, or wrongly reasoned.

The Vocabulary 223

catachresis

a strained, awkward usage of a word or phrase, commonly committed when one is straining for an effect rather than speaking plainly.

dehort

to urge against an action; the opposite of "exhort." (This is an indisputably obsolete word, out of usage since the Middle Ages, but it is included here both to explain Arthur Greenwood's little passage, above, in the definition for *secern,* and to end this book on a truly obscure note!)

Index of Vocabulary Words

A

abattoir, 219
abeyance, 145
abject, 92
abjure, 93
ablution, 85
abnegate, 28
aboulia, 200
abrogate, 105
abstemious, 63
abstruse, 93
abulia, 200
abysmal, 111
academe, 25
accede, 65
accouterments, 27
accoutrements, 27
accretion, 146
acerbic, 41
acidulous, 193
acquiescent, 78
acrimonious, 26
acropper, 220
acuity, 69
adamantine, 190
adduce, 95
adjure, 187
adroit, 35
advert, 175
aerie, 132
affable, 90
afflatus, 42
agon, 193
alacrity, 44

alarum, 112
alcahest, 220
alembic, 173
alexandrine, 167
alkahest, 220
allay, 62
allusion, 20
altercation, 33
altumal, 207
amanuensis, 139
amatory, 113
ambit, 186
amenable, 52
amerce, 185
amphoric, 120
analecta, 119
analects, 119
analeptic, 111
anapaest, 120
anapest, 120
ancien regime, 150
ancillary, 136
andante, 198
androgynous, 102
anent, 122
angst, 29
anile, 197
animus, 81
annotation, 133
annunciatory, 90
anodyne, 88
anomaly, 96
antecedent, 39
anthroposophy, 179
antinomian, 196
antipathy, 98

antiphon, 206
apercu, 150
apnea, 66
apodictic, 181
apogee, 53
apostasy, 53
apostolic, 42
apostrophe, 97
apothegm, 171
apotheosis, 49
apotheym, 137
append, 94
apperception, 130
apposite, 48
apprise, 52
apprize, 176
approbation, 142
aprication, 205
apterous, 115
arcane, 55
archaism, 184
argent, 174
argot, 163
argus, 155
armature, 197
arrant, 169
arrogate, 136
artificer, 81
ascetic, 26
ascribe, 53
asinine, 47
asperity, 119
asperse, 119
aspirate, 116
asseverate, 132
assiduous, 98
assuage, 76
ataraxia, 217
atavism, 110
athwart, 74
atrabilious, 130
augur, 79
auscultation, 192
auspicate, 196
auspicious, 88
austere, 32
avatar, 73
aver, 68

azoic, 160

B

bacchante, 147
badinage, 58
bagatelle, 132
bailiwick, 139
baleful, 162
ballista, 187
banal, 61
banausic, 178
barbican, 209
basilisk, 190
bathos, 61
batrachian, 144
bawd, 163
bedizened, 198
beg, 101
beleaguer, 27
bellicose, 76
bemused, 32
benighted, 152
benignant, 20
benison, 221
beseech, 122
beset, 84
bespoke, 99
bibulous, 118
bight, 107
billet, 148
bistre, 131
blandishment, 67
blase, 77
blithe, 72
blithesome, 72
bloviate, 129
blowsy, 140
blowzy, 140
boltered, 202
bombastic, 115
bowdlerize, 157
bridle, 87
brigand, 113
brinkmanship, 170
brio, 128
bruit, 109
brummagem, 158

buncombe, 158
bunkum, 158

C

cabal, 25
cabalistic, 25
cacophonus, 39
caesura, 185
calcined, 182
callipygian, 171
calumnious, 22
camorra, 172
canaille, 23
canard, 71
canicular, 196
canon, 67
canonize, 45
cant, 89
canthus, 113
capabarre, 209
capricious, 23
captious, 90
caracole, 220
carmine, 120
castellan, 210
casuistry, 95
catachresis, 224
cataleptic, 217
catholicon, 210
caveat, 93
cavil, 90
celerity, 113
censure, 115
cerement, 194
cerise, 210
charlatan, 93
charnel, 196
chasten, 91
chattel, 83
chauvinism, 80
chauvinist, 60
chilblain, 161
chilblains, 161
chiliast, 212
chimerical, 120
chrysalis, 190
churlish, 37

circumflex, 155
clamant, 218
clangor, 126
claudication, 159
clerisy, 212
cloy, 82
clyster, 201
codocil, 31
coercion, 72
coeval, 116
cogent, 81
cognate, 183
cognoscenti, 129
colloquy, 103
comminatory, 217
commingle, 121
comminuted, 117
compendious, 127
compendium, 157
complacent, 77
complaisant, 77
compline, 167
comportment, 47
conatus, 173
concierge, 122
concinnity, 124
concinuity, 124
concomitant, 123
concrescence, 124
concupiscence, 122
condign, 117
conducive, 109
confect, 198
conflate, 130
congener, 191
congeries, 161
connivent, 135
conniving, 42
consanguine, 210
consist, 207
consonant, 123
constuprate, 216
contiguity, 47
contravene, 135
contretemps, 136, 174
contrite, 111
contumacy, 28
contumely, 60

Index 229

conturbation, 195
conundrum, 97
conurbation, 195
conventicle, 198
co-opt, 87
coot, 45
copse, 91
coriaceous, 206
corposant, 123
cortege, 126
coruscate, 189
corvine, 116
costive, 201
coterie, 38
cozen, 215
crapulent, 202
crapulous, 202
craven, 74
crenulated, 126
crepitate, 155
crepuscular, 145
cretin, 66
crotchet, 159
cryptic, 22
cuirass, 158
culpable, 38
cumbrous, 132
cunctation, 164
cuneiform, 177
cupidity, 102
curmudgeon, 66
cynosure, 103

D

daedal, 203
darksome, 188
dauphin, 175
de facto, 68
de jure, 68
debar, 112
debouchment, 174
decalogue, 189
decimate, 59
declaim, 128
decollete, 127
décollete, 127
decretal, 184

decry, 106
defalcation, 100
defenestration, 121
dégagé, 208
dehort, 224
deign, 79
dejections, 220
deliquescent, 190
delusive, 70
demarch, 169
demesne, 204
demivierge, 181
demotic, 188
demulcent, 201
demur, 31
demure, 31
dengue, 170
denigrate, 34
denouement, 24
deprecate, 103
depredate, 37
derisive, 104
derisory, 34
descant, 170
descry, 106
deshabille, 200
despiciency, 147
desultory, 53
deus ex machina, 81
devolve, 65
diadem, 138
diapason, 163
diaspora, 115
didactic, 105
diffident, 21
dilettante, 83
discalced, 222
disconsolate, 86
dishabille, 200
disingenuous, 84
disparate, 77
disport, 154
disquisition, 48
dissemble, 119
dissimulate, 119
dissolute, 78
dithyramb, 189
divagation, 210

divertissement, 114
djinn, 216
dolmen, 223
dolor, 191
dolorous, 113
doppelganger, 194
doss, 183
dotage, 139
doyen, 142
draconian, 169
draconic, 177
droxy, 183
dualism, 107
dudgeon, 114
dulcet, 71
dun, 53
dyadic, 183
dysgenic, 94
dyspeptic, 64

E

ebriety, 176
ebullient, 23
ecchymotic, 180
eclectic, 30
educe, 114
efface, 27
effete, 36
efficacity, 45
efficacy, 45
effluvia, 105
effulgence, 61
effusive, 104
egalitarian, 121
egest, 162
egregious, 102
eleemosynary, 215
elegiac, 32
elision, 131
elysium, 183
elytra, 180
embassage, 222
embonpoint, 180
embouchure, 130
embrasure, 131
emendation, 141
emir, 176

emolument, 149
empiric, 205
empirical, 104
emprise, 142
empyrean, 177
emulous, 140
emunctory, 199
enchase, 124
encomiast, 148
encomium, 149
enervate, 78
enfeoff, 179
enfetter, 119
enfilade, 199
engender, 85
enigmatic, 20
enmity, 80
ennui, 100
ensconced, 89
entail, 82
entreat, 187
entreaty, 40
enure, 71
ephemeral, 46
epicene, 146
epicure, 96
epiphany, 30
eponymous, 125
equable, 89
equipoise, 47
eristic, 175
eristical, 175
ersatz, 107
erstwhile, 42
eructation, 192
erudite, 109
eschatological, 42
eschew, 45
esculent, 208
esoteric, 22
espial, 194
espy, 106
estivate, 166
esurient, 22
etiolate, 168
etiology, 190
eudaemon, 196
eudemon, 196

Index 231

evanescent, 44
evince, 141
exacerbate, 28
excrescence, 114
exculpatory, 38
excurse, 137
execration, 123
exegesis, 133
exigencies, 50
exiguous, 53
exordium, 180
expedient, 91
expiate, 73
explodent, 156
exposit, 123
expurgate, 157
extemporaneous, 67
extemporary, 67

F

fabliau, 188
facetious, 29
factious, 78
factitious, 55
factotum, 169
farouche, 209
fascicle, 168
fastness, 127
fatamorgana, 156
fatuous, 134
favonian, 189
febrile, 170
feckless, 82
feculent, 209
fecund, 26
festal, 144
fetor, 208
fetter, 90
fetters, 90
feuilleton, 157
fey, 129
fictive, 125
filiate, 213
fillip, 212
fissiparous, 200
flack, 202
flagitous, 142

flavid, 153
fleer, 218
flummox, 66
foment, 99
foofaraw, 171
fractious, 129
friable, 133
frigor, 221
frigorific, 178
frippery, 221
frisson, 140
froward, 203
frowsty, 206
fubsy, 137
fugacious, 165
fugal, 158
fuggy, 135
fulgor, 144
fuliginous, 159
fulminate, 176
fulsome, 113
fulvous, 112
furtive, 92
fustian, 176

G

gabble, 70
gadarene, 179
gadfly, 68
galvanic, 134
galvanizing, 134
gambol, 40
gaminish, 159
gasconade, 172
gelid, 182
gentry, 72
genuflexion, 153
gesticulate, 33
gibbous, 181
gimcrack, 144
gimlet, 126
glabella, 178
glabrous, 216
glaucous, 173
gloam, 153
gloze, 151
glozening, 189

glyptic, 214
gnosis, 156
gobbet, 168
goodish, 138
gormless, 211
gouache, 114
gratuitous, 95
grimoire, 219
guile, 108
gules, 180
gulosity, 174
gustative, 137
gustatory, 137
guy, 222

H

habitude, 187
hackneyed, 39
halcyon, 46
hale, 221
harangue, 73
harridan, 175
haute, 198
hector, 147
hegemony, 149
hegira, 213
hejira, 213
heterodox, 95
hiatus, 97
hieratic, 203
hierophant, 179
hind, 195
histrionic, 102
hoary, 116
homiletic, 162
Horla, 221
hortatory, 59
houri, 211
hoyden, 87
hubris, 80
hustings, 158

I

iambic, 48
ichor, 187
iconoclastic, 31

iconographic, 116
iconography, 69
icterus, 177
ictus, 117
idoneous, 204
illimitude, 64
immanent, 117
imminent, 56
immure, 85
impalpable, 115
imperium, 93
implacable, 102
impone, 79
importune, 43
impost, 203
impostume, 209
imprecate, 43
impudent, 96
impugn, 80
impunity, 85
impute, 64
inamorata, 194
inane, 96
inanition, 145
incarnadine, 152
incertitude, 105
inchoate, 55
incipient, 55
incondite, 192
increate, 217
inculcate, 122
inculpate, 124
incult, 124
indefatigable, 52
indemnify, 110
indissoluble, 73
indolent, 24
indurated, 127
ineffable, 100
ineluctable, 21
inexorable, 33
inflorescence, 122
ingenuous, 83
ingratiating, 101
inhere, 51
inimical, 75
iniquity, 68
innocuous, 56

Index 233

inquorate, 214
inscrutable, 34
insensate, 67
insentient, 57
insidious, 109
insipid, 57
insouciant, 56
instauration, 153
insular, 141
intercalate, 107
interdict, 162
internecine, 50
interregnum, 134
intestine, 184
intrigant, 182
inure, 71
inutile, 154
invective, 79
inveigh, 39
inveigle, 39
inveterate, 88
invidious, 109
invigilate, 215
involution, 216
inwit, 193
irascible, 45
irenic, 198
iridescent, 117
irrefragable, 205

J

jaded, 77
janissary, 175
jaundiced, 57
jejune, 51
jeremiad, 68
jerkwater, 128
jingoism, 198
jocose, 176
jocular, 176
jocund, 176
juggernaut, 84

L

lachrymal, 115
laconic, 46

lacuna, 182
lagniappe, 164
lapidary, 175
latibule, 208
laudatory, 88
leaven, 142
legerity, 114
leitmotif, 84, 180
lenitive, 164
lenity, 147
leonine, 132
leporine, 155
leviathan, 46
levity, 92
lexicon, 84
licentious, 145
lickerish, 207
lickerous, 207
lilt, 64
limicole, 208
limicoline, 208
limn, 106
lineament, 213
litany, 70
lithophanic, 153
litigious, 124
litterateur, 186
littoral, 164
liturgy, 120
loath, 22
loathe, 22
locus classicus, 215
logodaedaly, 156
loquacious, 63
loth, 22
lubricious, 173
lubricity, 153
lucubration, 166
lucubrations, 166
luculent, 187
Lucullan, 158
ludic, 193
lugubrious, 103
lumpen, 199
lurid, 93
lustrum, 142
lutanist, 152
lycanthropy, 218

M

maculate, 220
madeleine, 127
maenad, 177
magniloquent, 63
maieutic, 168
malaise, 152
maleficent, 121
malign, 20
mammothrept, 201
manna, 44
manqué, 151
mansuetude, 209
martinet, 151
matutinal, 165
maudlin, 107
maunder, 159
mawkish, 129
meliorate, 143
meliorism, 143
mellifluous, 145
memorious, 219
mendacious, 72
mendacity, 111
meninx, 183
mensuration, 183
meretricious, 89
midden, 161
minacious, 205
minatory, 205
minikin, 157
misanthrope, 97
miscegenate, 26
miscreant, 65
misericord, 171
misogynistic, 66
misogynous, 66
misology, 184
missish, 206
mistral, 167
moiety, 56
moil, 193
molder, 223
monody, 151
mordant, 41
morganatic, 196
moribund, 31
morose, 87
mortmain, 160
mufti, 143
mumchance, 206
murid, 197
murrain, 197
must, 152
myrmidon, 205
mythopeic, 178
mythopoeic, 178

N

nabob, 165
nacreous, 134
naif, 75
nates, 191
natter, 170
nebulous, 92
necrotic, 129
neoteric, 188
nepenth, 207
nepenthe, 207
neuralgic, 192
neurasthenia, 136
nexus, 52
nictitate, 39
nimbus, 112
nodose, 172
noetic, 172
nominal, 104
nonce, 122
nonpareil, 146
nostrum, 186
noumenal, 156
nugatory, 185
numinous, 135

O

obdurate, 49
obeisance, 194
obelize, 223
obfuscate, 82
objurgatory, 197
oblate, 166
oblations, 166
obloquy, 160

obmutescence, 213
obsequious, 45
obstreperous, 63, 90
obtain, 37
obtest, 146
obtrude, 73
obtrusive, 101
obverse, 133
obviate, 95
oculate, 192
odalisk, 137
odalisque, 137
odeum, 143
odium, 143
odorous, 57
oeuvre, 84
officious, 52
oleaginous, 160
onerous, 27
opalescent, 120
opine, 74
opprobrium, 110
ordure, 141
orison, 172
ormolu, 177
orotund, 158
ostensible, 106
ostensive, 106
ostentatious, 40
otiose, 111
outré, 176
ovine, 182
oxymoron, 71

P

paean, 47
paladin, 153
palatinate, 149
palaver, 62
palimpsest, 173
palladium, 185
palliate, 124
pallid, 62
palpate, 121
panache, 30
pandect, 184
pander, 70

panoply, 163
panoptic, 214
pantheon, 69
Paraclete, 181
paradigm, 24
paragon, 24
paralogism, 139
parlous, 19
paroxysm, 41
parse, 67
parterre, 182
parvenu, 137
pastiche, 189
patois, 69
patrin, 223
patronymic, 120
patteran, 223
peccant, 165
peculator, 23
pedagogic, 83
pedantic, 83
peevish, 135
pejorative, 105
Pelagianism, 198
pellucid, 21
pensile, 155
pensum, 150
penury, 147
percipient, 36
perdition, 49
peregrine, 54
peremptory, 35
perfervid, 183
perfidiuous, 99
perforce, 54
perfunctory, 44
peripatetic, 63
peripeteia, 209
peripety, 209
peristyle, 156
pernicious, 96
peroration, 78
perpend, 104
perquisite, 94
persiflage, 132
perspicacious, 28
perspicuous, 28
pertinacious, 30

pervasive, 98
pestiferous, 64
pettish, 140
petulant, 56
phalanx, 125
phantasm, 108
pharmacopoea, 174
philippic, 163
philistine, 67
phiz, 165
phlegmatic, 58
phocine, 189
physiognomy, 133
picaresque, 43
pied, 202
pique, 100
piractical, 205
piratical, 205
placate, 20
plangent, 111
plashy, 218
platitude, 34
plenary, 186
pleonasm, 175
plica, 178
pneuma, 195
poesy, 145
polemic, 117
polemicize, 35
polity, 46
poltroon, 19
polymathic, 159
porcine, 194
portentous, 116
postern, 203
postprandial, 161
postulant, 123
pother, 164
pottle, 151
pravity, 193
precipitous, 52
precis, 157
predilection, 85
preempt, 35
prefect, 33
preprandial, 192
presage, 79
prescient, 63

prescind, 168
prest, 43
prestidigitation, 43
presumptuous, 99
pretentious, 100
preternatural, 140
prevaricate, 92
prevenient, 197
priapic, 154
primogeniture, 185
probity, 81
proclivity, 26
Procrustean, 171
prodigal, 75
prodrom, 208
prodrome, 208
profligate, 54
profundity, 35
prolix, 141
promulgate, 28
propaedeutic, 184
propine, 132
propitiate, 34
propitious, 105
prorogue, 148
proscenium, 222
protean, 113
protreptic, 136
Proustian, 120
provenance, 87
provenience, 199
prurient, 25
pucka, 221
puckish, 167
puerility, 108
puffery, 27
puisne, 147
puissance, 86
pukka, 221
pule, 208
puling, 157
pullulate, 165
punctilious, 57
pundit, 48
purblind, 201
purdah, 191
purl, 125
purlieu, 126

Index 237

purling, 156
pusillanimous, 19
pustulate, 48
putative, 29
putsch, 114

Q

quatrain, 121
querulous, 23
quid pro quo, 41
quiddity, 40
quiescent, 63
quintessence, 96
quodlibet, 151
quotidian, 118

R

racemose, 121
rachitic, 191
raconteur, 101
radix, 132
raffish, 155
raiment, 65
rancor, 88
rantipole, 207
rapine, 135
ratiocinate, 118
rebuke, 89
recalcitrant, 104
recondite, 81
recrement, 200
recriminations, 54
recrudescence, 107
rectitude, 104
recumbent, 140
recusant, 123
recuse, 128
redolent, 98
redound, 69
redress, 148
refulgence, 61
regnant, 139
relict, 200
reliquary, 172
reluct, 173
remand, 66

remise, 156
remonstrate, 76
remunerate, 77
renascence, 60
rencounter, 82
repine, 185
replete, 62
reprehensible, 55
reproach, 59
reprobate, 122
reprove, 66
rescision, 148
restive, 58
reticent, 98
reticulate, 94
revenant, 140
revile, 109
riant, 217
rictus, 131
rife, 64
rill, 125
rime, 119
risible, 167
rive, 54
roborant, 146
rotary, 150
rotogravure, 195
rousant, 123
rubicund, 144
rubric, 68
ruction, 213
rufous, 154

S

sacrosanct, 96
sagacious, 69
salacious, 26
salient, 38
sanative, 23
sanctimonious, 108
sang-froid, 75
sanguine, 92
Sanhedrin, 162
sapient, 101
sapphic, 173
sardonic, 109
satrapy, 170

saturnine, 133
scabrous, 125
scansion, 189
scaraboid, 116
scatological, 171
scelerate, 204
scend, 207
schadenfreude, 128
sciolism, 169
sciolist, 181
scrannel, 138
scrivener, 166
scrobiculate, 143
scrofulous, 51
scrupulous, 135
scrutator, 150
scudding, 177
secern, 223
sectary, 202
seditious, 33
seigneur, 211
sejant, 131
seminal, 71
sempiternal, 199
seneschal, 210
sententious, 41
sepulture, 144
seraglio, 191
sere, 194
serried, 61
shibboleth, 94
shieling, 204
sibilant, 118
simulacrum, 154
sinecure, 103
siwash, 223
slat, 220
slattern, 125
sobriquet, 164
solecism, 174
solicitous, 134
solipsism, 110
solon, 199
somnambulant, 52
sonority, 86
sonorous, 76
sophistry, 44
sordid, 27

sortilege, 201
sough, 167
soupcon, 169
sparge, 172
spavined, 181
spindrift, 165
splenetic, 19
spoliate, 145
spurious, 105
stanch, 114
steatopygian, 171
stertorous, 186
straiten, 180
stultify, 162
subfusc, 213
sublunary, 161
suborn, 177
subtile, 160
subvention, 217
succinct, 79
succor, 134
sui generis, 112
supercilious, 60
supererogate, 204
supererogatory, 160
supernumary, 189
supernumerary, 189
suppliant, 182
supplicate, 122
suppositious, 170
surd, 179
surety, 138
surreptitious, 108
suspiration, 182
susurrous, 161
suzerain, 165
swarthy, 99
swinge, 206
sybaritic, 32
sycophant, 78
sylvan, 94
syncope, 203
syncretic, 212
syncretism, 166
syndicalism, 190
synecdoche, 130

Index 239

T

tableau, 86
tacit, 59
taciturn, 59
talus, 155
teleological, 219
telluric, 219
temerity, 29
temporize, 61
tenable, 97
tendentious, 74
tendresse, 188
tenebrious, 144
tenebrous, 144
tenuous, 25
tergiversate, 147
termagant, 30
terse, 79
thanatos, 211
thaumaturge, 204
theriomorphic, 179
thrall, 110
threnody, 211
titivate, 204
titubation, 159
tocsin, 195
tonsure, 163
tope, 143
topiary, 132
torose, 138
torpid, 72
torpor, 47
tortuous, 108
torus, 139
touchstone, 40
traduce, 70
tranche, 214
transmogrify, 49
travails, 158
travesty, 25
trenchant, 58
trepidation, 57
trice, 74
trichoid, 143
trite, 36
trope, 141
truckle, 169
truculent, 58
trull, 178
tsigane, 155
tumefy, 124
tumescent, 80
tumid, 146
turbid, 62
turpid, 153
tutoyer, 151

U

ukase, 164
ululation, 191
umbrage, 37
unctious, 31
unctuous, 31
undine, 152
untrammeled, 59
uranist, 188
ursine, 170
usufruct, 157
usurp, 87
uxorious, 187

V

vacuity, 112
vagaries, 126
valetudinarian, 152
vapid, 23
variegate, 136
varisized, 153
vassal, 149
vaticinate, 201
vaunt, 137
vectress, 200
vehement, 86
velleity, 146
velutinous, 200
venal, 70
venery, 192
venial, 70
ventricose, 215
veracious, 65
veracity, 65
verbose, 24
verdure, 65

veridical, 195
verisimilitude, 38
vernal, 105
verst, 115
vertiginous, 117
vet, 82
viands, 175
viatic, 154
vibracy, 118
vibrancy, 118
vicarious, 83
vilify, 36
violaceous, 104
virago, 103
virescence, 64
viridity, 212
virulent, 76
viscid, 187
vitiate, 72
vitriolic, 37
vituperative, 73

vivacious, 24
voluble, 24
vouchsafe, 99

W

warren, 138
weal, 149
whilom, 42
wight, 166
wrack, 218

X

xenophobia, 147

Z

zeitgeist, 128

www.ingramcontent.com/pod-product-compliance
Lightning Source LLC
Chambersburg PA
CBHW032106090426
42743CB00007B/256